# THE ART OF
# Changing Course

# THE ART OF
# Changing
# Course

**A 3-Step Strategy to Get Unstuck
and Solve Your Real Problems**

# CHRIS RUDEN

WILEY

Published by John Wiley & Sons, Inc., Hoboken, New Jersey.
Published simultaneously in Canada.

For general information on our other products and services or for technical support, please contact our Customer Care Department within the United States at (800) 762-2974, outside the United States at (317) 572-3993 or fax (317) 572-4002. Wiley also publishes its books in a variety of electronic formats. Some content that appears print may not be available in electronic formats. For more information about Wiley products, visit our web site at www.wiley.com.

*Library of Congress Cataloging-in-Publication Data Is Available:*

ISBN 9781394247660 (Cloth)
ISBN 9781394247677 (ePub)
ISBN 9781394253494 (ePDF)
ISBN 9781394308606 (oBook)

COVER DESIGN: PAUL MCCARTHY

SKY10079634_071724

*To my beautiful life partner, Paula. In this life and 1,000 others, it will always be you. Thank you for being my #1 fan and lending me your belief when I've run out of my own. I know you said to never call you up on stage as you'd probably croak, so here is my compromise.*

*—Love, Chrustopher*

# Contents

Foreword      ix

Introduction      3

Chapter 1    What's the Problem?      17

Chapter 2    Why Haven't You Addressed It Yet?      27

Chapter 3    The Power of Language      41

Chapter 4    Prescription to Change      63

Chapter 5    See It, Face It, Fix It      75

Chapter 6    Step 1: Subconscious to Conscious      83

Chapter 7    Step 2: Conscious to Communicated      105

Chapter 8    Step 3: Communicated to Broadcast      135

Chapter 9    Real-World Application      167

Chapter 10    Accepting Feedback (without Letting It Defeat You)      179

# Contents

**Chapter 11  Overcoming Pitfalls**                187

**Chapter 12  Mentoring Others**                   199

**References**                                      207

**About the Author**                                209

**Index**                                           211

# Foreword

When Chris approached me to pen the foreword for his book, I was overwhelmed by a whirlwind of emotions: gratitude, excitement, and yes, even tears. You might wonder about the tears—they stemmed from the profound privilege of witnessing Chris's journey toward authentic confidence. It's a journey that has profoundly affected my life and one that I'm deeply honored to articulate in this opening page.

I'm Mindy Scheier, a fashion designer by trade, and also the proud mother of a son with muscular dystrophy. My quest began when my son Oliver simply yearned to wear jeans like his peers—a seemingly simple desire complicated by his inability to manage buttons, zippers independently, or accommodate leg braces. I was astounded by the lack of mainstream, stylish, and functional clothing options. Thus, armed with my background, I embarked on a "modest" mission to revolutionize the fashion industry. In 2014, the Runway of Dreams Foundation was born. Our mission? To educate the fashion world about the significance of including people with disabilities in the conversation—not just as consumers, but as integral voices shaping the industry's future. In 2016, our partnership with Tommy Hilfiger marked a historic milestone: creating the first-ever mainstream Adaptive clothing line. Yet, to truly make waves in the fashion world, we knew we had to step onto the grand stage of New York Fashion Week, showcasing Adaptive apparel through groundbreaking runway shows spotlighting models with disabilities. Our journey led us beyond NYC, with our sights set on Las Vegas.

I vividly recall meeting Chris for the first time, as he prepared to grace the runway in our Las Vegas show. His infectious smile illuminated the room, instantly forging connections with the diverse array of models with varying disabilities. It was a sight to behold. Beneath his vibrant exterior, Chris harbored a sense of trepidation—a fear born from unfamiliarity with both the runway and the shared experience of countless individuals with disabilities, being vulnerable in new situations. Reflecting on the show, Chris confided in me: "It was exhilarating yet nerve-racking. But the rapid sense of connection, the over-whelming support, and the profound inclusivity I experienced were unlike anything I'd ever known. To feel celebrated and embraced in a world that often felt exclusive was truly eye-opening." His words have stayed with me since, a testament to Chris's indomitable spirit.

In 2019, I embarked on another venture: GAMUT Manage-ment, a consultancy and talent community exclusively for people with disabilities that helps companies find authentic ways to engage with, create products for, and represent people with disabilities both internally and externally. One of the first people I called to come join GAMUT was Chris. Without hesi-tation, he embraced the opportunity to amplify not only his voice but all voices of people with disabilities, recognizing the seismic impact of their perspectives on any industry finally willing to listen. This encapsulates the magic of Chris.

As someone who has dedicated my life to making change happen in our mainstream world, I firmly believe in the art of changing course. Chris exemplifies this artistry, offering a bea-con of hope to those navigating life's tumultuous waters. His story resonates deeply for anyone grappling with upheavals of any kind, reminding us that resilience, adaptability, and deter-mination can conquer even the most daunting challenges.

Chris's narrative underscores the transformative power of change management. Through perseverance and unwavering resolve, he has surmounted seemingly insurmountable obsta-cles, inspiring countless individuals to do the same. In today's rapidly evolving landscape, mastering the art of change is imperative—personally, professionally, and organizationally. By embracing change, we unlock boundless potential, propelling ourselves toward greater heights of success and fulfillment. And in Chris, we find not just a teacher of change management, but an embodiment of its essence—a testament to the triumph of the human spirit.

Thank you, Chris, for this privilege and honor. You are a gifted storyteller, and I'm proud to call you a friend. To those about to turn the page, enjoy the journey.

With tremendous respect and admiration,
Mindy Scheier
Founder and CEO, GAMUT Management and Runway of Dreams Foundation

"He who rejects change is the architect of decay. The only human institution which rejects progress is the cemetery."

—*Harold Wilson*

**Coroner:** She's really, most sincerely dead.

**Mayor:** Then this is a day of independence for all the Munchkins and their descendants!

**Barrister:** If any!

**Mayor:** Yes, let the joyous news be spread.

**Mayor:** The Wicked Old Witch at last is dead!

**Munchkins:** (sing) Ding Dong! The Witch is dead. Which old witch? The Wicked Witch! Ding Dong! The Wicked Witch is dead!

# Introduction

There's an old saying that goes, "Be like the wind and change with ease and without contempt."

The only problem is that you're *not* wind, and change is *not* that easy.

Philosophically, change is the only constant in life, so you'd think it would be relatively easy to master over time. Yet, change remains one of the most difficult recurrences in life.

From growing up and no longer being able to eat chicken nuggets every day to navigating corporate mergers and everything in between, change is constant.

And it can be exhausting at times.

Twelve-year-old me wanted nothing more than to be a veterinarian.

Seventeen-year-old me would have joined the military if he didn't have diabetes.

Nineteen-year-old me knew he would become a lawyer.

Twenty-two-year-old me graduated with an exercise science degree.

Twenty-seven-year-old me stopped hiding his disability.

Thirty-year-old me built a professional speaking business on change.

Thirty-three-year-old me still loves chicken nuggets.

You could say changing course is my forte, but to be honest, I've been forced to change course many times—positive changes and negative changes, internal changes and external changes—and it took me a long time to learn how to navigate change effectively.

**Unless you're dead, you've also experienced change. And if you're living, you will continue to experience change.**

While change is constant, there is an art to it. I believe that our ability to adapt (or not) to our evolving needs determines our quality of outcomes and quality of life.

You can adapt to the changes that are happening, or you can adapt in order to change yourself. Both reacting to change and initiating change are skills that can be improved that set you up for effective choices as life changes or you find yourself needing to change the direction your life is heading.

Whether you like it or not, you will become a master of change reaction. You either become really good at it or really bad at it. Or you simply master not changing at all. A choice is always made whether you react effectively or ineffectively—whether you act or do nothing at all. Navigating unfamiliar territory such as health, financial, and relationship changes along with any other disruptive events that range from uncomfortable to traumatic will influence your path in life. That influence, depending on your change management resolve, will be the wind guiding your boat either to the shore or the rocks.

Reacting to change is not the only disruptive force you need to prepare to manage, though.

Sometimes, you might find yourself *wanting* to change—maybe even needing to change. Not necessarily because of some sort of cataclysmic event but rather a realization that the track you're on or the actions you are taking are no longer serving you. And as you think about it, maybe they never did.

What could be worse than realizing you're no longer happy or fulfilled in one or more areas of your life? Realizing you know you haven't been happy with those areas for years so you mastered the reaction by inaction, leaving you feeling stuck.

"Something has got to change," you say to yourself.

When that happens, it's usually because you're experiencing some sort of pain or lack of contentment or progress that makes you wish for something different for yourself.

No matter what you're looking to change, pain points act as catalysts, motivating change to alleviate discomfort, dissatisfaction, or challenges.

Conversely, "desire points" represent the aspirations, goals, and positive outcomes you're looking to achieve through change. They also can serve as drivers to help maneuver you through the stuck inertia.

You will always react to change in some way. But you might not always initiate the change you want. You will undoubtedly find yourself needing to become your own pattern disruptor if you ever genuinely want the pattern that no longer serves you to be disrupted.

Reacting to change has to do with how you perceive change (threat vs opportunity), the lens through which you view change (negative, positive, or neutral), and your urgency to act accordingly.

Not all who react well to change initiate change for themselves.

So if you're living with pain or a desire to change or you're just flat out exhausted keeping your head barely above water in areas of your life that don't fulfill you, I'm going to ask you a very difficult question:

**Why haven't you done anything about it yet?**

**What the stuck?**

The one common thread among situations calling for change is "stuckness." At the cusp of change is a deep, innate desire to maintain familiarity.

People defend their familiarity by staying stuck in a place that no longer serves them, whether that is a relationship that should've ended years ago, a dream that should've been pursued, or an organization failing to innovate because it wants to stay the same.

Sameness is stuckness.

Feeling stuck used to send me in a spiral, frustrated to the point of inaction. After all, nothing is worse than feeling stuck in a situation where you hoped you would succeed.

This book aims to help you navigate change to alter your course from stuckness to reinvention by turning uncertainty into clarity. Your needs evolve. Your circumstances change. What once excited you might cause you heartburn now.

Maybe you've lost that inner flame you once had. Maybe your mental health has started to suffer due to your values and aspirations being disjointed from your current life.

And maybe—just maybe—you know there has to be more to life (and more you can give to life) than what you are currently experiencing.

This process, if you allow it, will help you to "unstuck" yourself. For good.

Maybe you're thinking that this all sounds great, but you're being forced to deal with some sort of disruptive change. Losing a job, a relationship ending, car breaking down, etc., are all examples of external disruptive change.

How do you intentionally manage disruptive changes like these? It can seem that you don't have a choice when external circumstances disrupt your plan or comfort. The natural response is to dwell on how terrible or inconvenient the change is. Without negating or invalidating natural feelings, there comes a point where labeling a disruption *good* or *bad* does nothing for you. At a certain point, it is up to you to stop describing the disruption and start managing it in a way that helps you rather than hurts you. Not wanting to change does not shield you from events outside of your control. When situations change, you respond. And that response will be either effective or ineffective. External change acts on you, but that is not the only disruptive force of change.

Sometimes, there is also the need to create your own disruptive change to break patterns and cycles that are not paying off for you. You find yourself needing to change an area of your life on your own, without the aid of some cataclysmic occurrence. From your health to wealth to relationships, we all fall in ruts and at times can feel trapped in a life we wish was just better. Despite the lack of fulfillment and results we crave, we sometimes go on autopilot, oblivious to the fact that the life we are choosing to repeat is not the life we want to lead. There will be times where you need a wake-up call. And that wake-up call might have to come from you.

Sometimes disruption is the best thing that can happen to you.

*The Art of Changing Course* applies to disruptive change. The Changing Course process, covered in this book, will help you learn how to handle disruptive change and use it as a catalyst to transform a passive autopilot life.

In most cases, you're stuck because you're afraid—you're not sure what to do—and your autopilot is on stuckness. That is a tough spot to be in because time vanishes when you are stuck on autopilot. Going from knowing you're stuck (aware) to not even thinking you're stuck anymore (unaware) sucks. When you normalize and accept being stuck, you live according to limitations that don't actually exist. Are you really stuck at that job? Are you really stuck with that mindset? Are you really stuck being who you are? Or are you just accepting something that you could actually change?

I believe that everyone should learn acceptance—except when you're stuck. Acceptance is necessary to make peace with what you cannot change—losing a loved one, changing the past, fear of the future, and so on. But when you accept something that you can change, you lie to yourself about what is possible. Accepting a lie is dangerous. I know because I was there for a long time, accepting that I needed to hide my disability forever.

Too many people accept their life for what it is, not realizing that they just have to make one step toward change.

Throughout this book, I'll be referring to parts of *The Wizard of Oz* storyline and character development to bring the examples to life.

Why? Because the classic tale, written by L. Frank Baum, is a great study of change management. If you've read the book or watched the 1939 film, you know that each character experiences change, and (spoiler alert), in the end, we learn that their solution is in their problem.

The task of traveling to see the wizard, which at first seems like a means to an end, actually becomes a transformative journey for Dorothy and her friends. *The Wizard of Oz* reinforces the idea that growth comes from facing our challenges and drawing upon our inner strengths instead of searching a sketchy yellow brick road for answers.

In the movie, we're able to see that each character obviously already has what they need without having to steal a broomstick or a pair of ruby slippers to get it.

If the scarecrow didn't have a brain, he obviously wouldn't be able to think or reason or communicate with Dorothy.

If the Tin Man didn't have a heart, he wouldn't be so sad about his situation.

If the lion didn't have courage, he wouldn't have been brave enough to make the journey to Oz.

A great leader allows people to be their own All Great and Powerful Oz.

A great leader exposes the good in the deficit.

And a great leader should know whether their people have a whole damn "ding dong the witch is dead" flash mob routine prepared for the day that they resign, retire, or get crushed by an airborne farmhouse.

So what can you expect from this book?

In simple terms, *The Art of Changing Course* is about learning how to effectively change course and get unstuck.

Change can definitely suck; don't get me wrong.

The real issue we have to deal with though is what sucks about change to *you?*

If you want to grow, you have to change. It's a fundamental truth of life.

**Some changes are easy and appealing ...**

- You get a raise. **Amazing.**
- You get to go on vacation to a place you've never been before. **Can't wait.**
- You get a lower interest rate on your mortgage. **Sweet.**

**Other types? Not so much ...**

- Something in your business is broken and needs to be fixed. **F*ck.**
- You can't fit into your favorite jeans. **F*ck.**
- A relationship is ending, and you don't want it to. **F*ck.**

And yet, we come back to that unavoidable fact: if you want to grow, you have to change.

We all have hurdles that need to be addressed as we move toward the life we desire.

Though many hurdles seem obvious, the true root of our problems often lurks in our subconscious minds and masquerades as a more superficial problem.

For example, I was born with a physical disability: I have only two fingers on my left hand, and my left arm is shorter than my right. I kept my hand buried in my pocket or hidden in a glove for the majority of my life, refusing to take ownership of the real problem: A fear of being alone. A fear of being judged. A fear of never being good enough. I imagined people being so put off by my arm that they wouldn't want to spend time with me.

After getting approved for a prosthetic arm, I decided to make a video and post it on YouTube. I went to sleep thinking maybe a few thousand people would see it. I woke up to find that it had been viewed millions of times. I received hundreds of emails from people who could relate to my message.

Each of those interactions made it easier for me to start showing up as the real version of myself instead of the false version I had been selling for so many years.

Now, I speak on stage to thousands of people all over the world, where I pull off my prosthetic and proudly raise my half-arm in the air for all to see.

I've been featured on Dwayne "The Rock" Johnson's hit TV show *Titan Games,* have had media coverage across huge platforms such as *Men's Health, The Washington Post,* and Netflix, and modeled for the likes of Tommy Hilfiger, Nike, and Zappos.

Over time, I codified my journey of owning both my physical disability and the emotional problem behind it into what is now the Changing Course process.

I share this process with organizations that want problem-solving frameworks and communication models they can apply to their situations and teams.

The Changing Course process is very intentionally elegant in its simplicity. I'm not here trying to sell you on a 12-part plan that you must follow for the rest of your life to get better or for your team to be more productive.

**Instead, I'm asking you to make three distinct shifts:**

- **Get honest** with yourself about whatever it is you need to change. (subconscious → conscious)
- **Be accountable** and share your commitments with people you trust and respect. (conscious → communicated)
- **Live by example** and operate daily as a better role model than you already are. (communicated → broadcast)

The Changing Course process is backed by a variety of psychological principles, management techniques, and organizational change theories, including Lewin's Three Step Model of Change, designed by psychologist Kurt Lewin, who was regarded as the intellectual father of organizational change (Burnes 2020).

Lewin's Three Step Model of Change suggests that sustainable transformations occur in three stages:

- **Unfreeze:** Accept that change is necessary, which mirrors the subconscious → conscious step.
- **Change:** Look for new ways to do things, which we find in the conscious → communicated step.
- **Refreeze:** Let the change sink in broadly and affect more people, which is what happens during the communicated → broadcast stage.

The Changing Course process works for just about any imaginable problem, from not feeling motivated at work to wanting to lose weight, from feeling unsatisfied in the place you live to not being sure whether you're in the right romantic relationship, or from managing employee churn to achieving income goals.

Most of us let these types of problems swim around in our heads and convince ourselves that, eventually, we'll arrive at an answer. In the meantime, all we're doing is elevating our own stress levels as these problems invade our subconscious.

**Most people have one core problem that, if solved, will fix a considerable amount of their other problems.**

The Changing Course process helps to solve *that* problem.

Here's how the process works:

## Step 1: Subconscious → Conscious

As an example of what this looks like in practice, one of the corporate clients I worked with was a Fortune 500 company that wanted their employees to be more culturally competent.

I asked them who in the company was responsible for diversity, equity, and inclusion (DEI).

Everyone pointed to Mary, the head of that department.

"Interesting," I said. "I thought everyone here was responsible for DEI."

The room was silent, but the message was loud.

I asked them to write down what they had personally done to further the goal of creating a more culturally competent office.

The leaders of the company *thought* their problem was the cultural competence of their employees. But the *real* problem was that they wanted something from other people that they weren't willing to do themselves.

People often think that doing nothing puts them in neutral territory, but the reality is that doing nothing can be just as problematic as doing the wrong thing.

## Step 2: Conscious → Communicated

Now that this leadership team knew they had a responsibility to improve the office culture, how could they own up to their missteps?

I encouraged them to speak with peers about times when they had overheard a joke or comment based on race, sex, or background and failed to shut it down. In sharing that vulnerable moment where they made a mistake, they also verbally committed to never letting that happen again. Instead of leadership telling what to do, they just communicated to them what they themselves plan to do as a personal commitment.

Leadership communicated a struggle they faced and took responsibility with resolve to fix it. That communication served as a pact of accountability.

Doing so also encouraged others to analyze their own actions and stop hiding the things that might have caused them inward shame. The leaders' ownership and authentic communication of their problems and commitment to act was reciprocated by the employees as well.

This move from conscious to communicated is the accountability phase of the Changing Course process. When the leaders let others know what they needed to work on, they were able to do so and do so together.


## Step 3: Communicated → Broadcast

Rather than relying on Mary to set policies and manage DEI initiatives by herself, each leader started speaking up when they saw negative and positive behaviors at the office.

In doing so, they were modeling that behavior to the rest of the company. They were publicly reclaiming their responsibility for providing a healthy, productive office and asserting their priorities to the entire organization.

Think about it like this: If you were in a room of 1,000 people and I asked you to stand up and start jumping around, you'd feel pretty uncomfortable. But if you go to a Tony Robbins seminar and the other 999 people in the room are jumping around, you'd feel weird if you stayed in your seat.

What we're doing with the Changing Course process is creating environments that are conducive to positive change. Whether that's your condo or your boardroom or your mind, creating better environments for change requires creating better habits for change. And creating better habits for change requires a plan that is simple:

Simple to start.

Simple to sustain.

Simple to stack.

With that company, like with all of my individual and corporate clients, I took the information they already knew and fed it to them in a digestible format so they could do something about it.

**My goal with this book is to help you do the same so you, too, can move from feeling overwhelmed to action.**

If you often feel exhausted trying to make change on your own or find yourself saying, "I don't have the skills for this" or "I'm a lazy person" or "I wish I could be more motivated," this book is for you.

But make no mistake, *The Art of Changing Course* is not a quick fix or a means to an end. It's the first step on your own personal yellow brick road journey to solve your problems toward the life you want to live.

Now it's time to make sure you're trying to solve the *right* problems.

> "People may spend their whole lives climbing the ladder of success only to find, once they reach the top, that the ladder is leaning against the wrong wall."
>
> —*Thomas Merton*

**Scarecrow:** How do you do?

**Dorothy:** Very well, thank you.

**Scarecrow:** Oh, I'm not feeling at all well. You see, it's very tedious being stuck up here all day long with a pole up your back.

**Dorothy:** Oh, dear—that must be terribly uncomfortable. Can't you get down?

**Scarecrow:** Down? No, you see, I'm—well—I'm—

**Dorothy:** Oh, well, here—let me help you.

**Scarecrow:** Oh, that's very kind of you—very kind.

**Dorothy:** Well, oh, dear—I don't quite see ...

**Dorothy:** o.s. ... how I can—

**Scarecrow:** Of course, I'm not bright about doing things, but if you'll just bend the nail down in the back, maybe I'll slip off and ...

# CHAPTER 1

# What's the Problem?

**KEY TASKS FROM THIS CHAPTER:**

- Think about the problem that's keeping you stuck, and determine if it's your *real* problem or a symptom of your real problem.
- Make a list of ways your life would be better if you solved that problem.

In 1945, Sears Roebuck Company made about one Taylor Swift Eras Tour ($1 billion) in revenue. (That would be the equivalent of $16 billion today.) By 1969, Sears' sales represented 1% of the US economy, and they were easily the largest retailer in the world. Sears employed 350,000 people and decided they needed to have one big fancy office space for their workforce.

Construction was completed on the Sears Tower in 1973. Standing at an impressive 1,454 feet, the Sears Tower became the tallest building in the world. And it maintained that record for 22 years.

One would think that global dominance would survive Walmart and the Internet, but apparently not. In 1991, Sears started losing market share when Walmart came along. They decided their problem was that they weren't big enough. So they merged with Kmart to try and create a larger retail footprint.

Sears's size wasn't the problem. Their problem was that they showed up too late for the digital game. By trying to get bigger, they just started to drown. More stores meant more overhead at a time when their competitors were figuring out how to be lean and agile by going online.

**Scaling an ineffective system leads to failure.**

It's like the time I ran over a nail and ended up with a punctured tire. Every morning I had to go out of my way to put air in it. I would then have enough air to last for a day. Then it would go low, I would have to fill it up again, and so on and so forth. To me, the problem was that I needed to go get air all the time. But the *real* problem was that I had a hole in my tire that had to be fixed.

Symptoms of the real problem can mask where your efforts need to go, leading to systems and processes being created that time and time again fail to deliver absolution. The problem, to me, transformed into blaming gas stations for not having working air hoses or not having Apple Pay because I didn't have any cash or quarters. I was late "because other people were filling up their tires" or "because two gas stations had broken tire inflation stations and one didn't have one at all."

My solution was to find better gas stations. I ignored and avoided the real problem and chose to deal with the consequential problems. But that was unnecessary.

Find the hole and patch the tire.

Getting to the core of the issue and assessing whether your answers are actually helping are really difficult to do though when you are committed to one course of unchecked action. We see this issue with scaling broken processes across America's transportation systems.

As populations increase, motorists increase. It seems only obvious to assume more motorists on the road create more traffic. So to solve the traffic debacle, more lanes would be needed to accommodate the motorists and eventually reduce and improve traffic, right?

But what if I told you adding more lanes not only does not improve traffic on roadways but actually, and even though it is counterintuitive, it contributes to even worse traffic?

The federal government has spent billions of dollars expanding highways and building bridges and overpasses in efforts to reduce traffic congestion. The efforts to lessen traffic, while appreciated (not the construction and delays due to the attempts to improve traffic by worsening it), are not factually sound. New roads, new lanes, and new expanded highways don't account for one thing—new driving. This feedback loop, known as *induced demand,* encourages drivers who normally avoided those congested roads to now use them. Induced demand is a concept that essentially states more resources for a problem might not necessarily solve the problem. Added roadway motivates more motorists to reroute, inevitably converting traffic on highways to more traffic on more highways.

Think about some of the largest highways in the United States: Los Angeles, Atlanta, Houston, New Jersey. Aerial shots of these 12- to 26-lane highways can hardly be found not in gridlocked traffic. The largest highway in the country, the

Katy Freeway in Houston, expanded to 26 lanes in 2008 and was praised as a success initially. But if economics has taught us anything, it's that when you provide a free beneficial resource, over time, that supply will not be able to keep up with demand. Five years after the widening of Katy Freeway, the *New York Times* reported, "Peak travel times were longer than before the expansion."

We're often too busy or overwhelmed or committed to our belief to see the bigger picture. But if we want to create or adapt to change, we have to dig deep and find the root of what it is that's keeping us stuck.

I didn't take the time to step back and look at the situation to see whether I was solving the right problem. And as a result, I was dealing with a by-product of the problem. That was keeping me frustrated and stuck and late for a lot of meetings.

Every single one of us has something in our life that we wish could be different ... like I wished my tire didn't need to be filled up with air all the time.

**One or two (or all) of these might be making you feel stuck:**

- A feeling of being unsatisfied in your work
- Experiencing burnout, stress, or lack of work–life balance
- Recognizing limited growth opportunities or stagnation
- Enduring frequent communication breakdowns or conflicts in relationships
- Feeling emotionally drained, undervalued, or underappreciated
- Discovering a lack of compatibility with a partner
- Health issues, chronic conditions, or physical discomfort
- Experiencing low energy, fatigue, or the inability to perform daily tasks
- The consequences of an unhealthy lifestyle

- Feeling stuck or lost in your life
- Dealing with fears, self-doubt, and/or a lack of confidence
- Financial instability
- Living paycheck to paycheck
- Overwhelming debt

The characters in *The Wonderful Wizard of Oz* teach us what happens when you stay stuck, and the amazing progress that comes when you break free from that stuckness. They were all putting air in the tire instead of patching it.

Maybe you want to be more physically fit. Maybe you're unhappy in your relationship. Maybe you would love to have a better job with a higher salary.

If you're like the majority of people I've worked with, there's usually one core issue that affects almost every area of your life and keeps you the same version of yourself year after year. This problem usually boils down to a deeper concept.

People *think* they want to lose weight, but what they're really seeking is the feeling that weight loss promises. If you lost 60 pounds but looked and felt the exact same, you wouldn't be happy.

Your problem is not necessarily that you need to find a new job. It's that you feel trapped by your current one; it's not giving you the financial freedom you seek.

Only when you recognize the root can you start to address the real problem.

For years, I kept my physical disability hidden away from the world. On a surface level, it would have seemed that not being able to show my hand was my core problem. But that didn't quite capture the issue. In reality, the problem I needed to address was a crippling fear of being alone. I had created a false narrative in my head that if I showed my hand, people would stop wanting to be around me. And I couldn't handle how that would feel.

As humans, we often treat feelings as facts.

Did you start thinking of your own problem as you read about mine? Or maybe you don't have a single thing in your life that you want to change. You may want to have a look at that, though, because there's a fine line between being stuck and being complacent.

Being stuck means you're repeating past mistakes despite knowing better. Being complacent is deciding things are good enough as they are.

True contentment, on the other hand, is the goal. It's about finding peace in whatever situation you're in. People who are genuinely content aren't stuck. They're in a state of acceptance and stability but derive continuing satisfaction from a sense of progress in life.

Deep down, you likely know what your real problem is— even if you haven't begun to address it yet. Whether it's understanding the roots of your problems or finding contentment in the journey, it's all about managing your perspective and your habits.

Change isn't about constant upheaval; it's about finding stability in both peace and chaos. It's recognizing that change happening and needing to change are both part of life so you need frameworks to manage it actively.

Let me ask you: How would you feel if you continued down the path you are currently on for the next six years? Yeah, you might get a raise or date people or take a few vacations. But what if you woke up six years from now and you were the same person on the inside as you are right now? Same mindset. Same view of the world. Same regrets. Just older.

Because you're reading this book, I will assume you wouldn't feel very good about that scenario.

The Greeks believed that "metabole," or change, is the general fate that awaits everything. From the smallest particles to the largest political parties to the constant chemical process of *metabolism* taking place in your body as you read this, change is everywhere.

Organisms undergo constant biochemical transformations to sustain life:

- Seeds to plants
- Plants to flowers
- Flowers to fruit
- Fruit to pie
- Carbohydrates into energy
- Fat into carbon dioxide (weight loss is mostly breathed out)
- Time into money
- Money into materials
- Hardship into story
- Obstacles to opportunities

We are in a constant evolution from state to state. And no state remains constant.

"You can never step in the same river twice."
—*Heraclitus*

**Before you move on to the next chapter, here are some questions to ask yourself to help uncover the real problem that's standing between you and the life you want:**

- What is the problem? (Clearly define the problem without making assumptions.)
- What are the specific issues causing the problem?
- What is the cause of this problem happening?
- Why is it a problem now if it wasn't before?
- Why is it a problem that needs to be solved?
- When does the problem come up? (Is it a constant issue, or does it happen at specific times? Does it occur under certain conditions?)
- Where does the problem come up for you? (Is the issue contained to a specific area of your life/business?)
- Who (if anyone) is involved or affected by the problem? (Identify the people or groups who would benefit by you solving this problem.)
- Are there specific people who play a role in this problem?
- How long has the problem been happening? (If you can figure out a timeline, you might have some clues to the root issue.)
- What have you already tried (if anything) to solve this problem?
- Can you identify any underlying factors contributing to the problem?
- Are there any patterns or trends surrounding this problem that could give you clues about when/why it comes up?

- What assumptions are you making about the problem? Are they all valid?
- What pieces of data would help you to understand the problem better? (Then go searching for them.)
- What are the consequences of not solving the real problem?
- What are the potential impacts and consequences of leaving this issue unaddressed?

**Scarecrow:** Here is a great tree, standing close to the ditch. If the Tin Woodman can chop it down, so that it will fall to the other side, we can walk across it easily.

**Lion:** That is a first-rate idea, one would almost suspect you had brains in your head, instead of straw.

# CHAPTER 2

# Why Haven't You Addressed It Yet?

**KEY TASKS FROM THIS CHAPTER:**

- List some possible unknown knowns that could be in your future and make a plan for dealing with them.
- Reverse-engineer your path.
- Think about where your ego might be keeping you stuck.
- Consider how anchoring bias can be keeping you from changing.
- Identify what is keeping you stuck and why you haven't addressed the issue yet.

Donald Rumsfeld was the US Secretary of Defense in 2002 when he delivered a news briefing that distinguished between the things we know (known knowns), the things we know we don't know (known unknowns), and the things we don't know we don't know (unknown unknowns).

He said, "If one looks throughout the history of our country and other free countries, it is the latter category that tends to be the difficult one" (Rumsfeld 2002).

Let's take a minute to break these down.

The Earth is round. Known known.

You're not sure how your audience will respond to a new product. Known unknown.

Global pandemic. Unknown unknown.

We're all familiar with unknown unknowns ... aka unexpected change. Unknown unknowns are tough to plan for because, well, we don't know they're coming. But of course we do. We will face unknown unknowns many times throughout our lives. So by being aware that unknown unknowns exist, we can prepare to be adaptable enough to navigate them.

If you're an organizational leader, part of what positioned you for the role was the knowledge and experience you've gathered up until now. However, knowledge is not enough to lead your team through change.

No one cares how much you know until they know how much you care. One way to show that you care is by shifting from a know-it-all mindset to a *learn-it all* mindset. Learn everything your employees need, fear, want, and struggle with. Learn what drives them and why they might be resistant to change. Learn about your resistance to change as well.

A learn-it-all leader guides their organization through change as its change champion. A know-it-all leader creates more resistance in an already unstable environment.

If you're in any leadership position—personally or professionally or both—embrace the reality that change is constant, and have a plan in place for the unexpected. This means being prepared to course correct in the face of change. Be vulnerable and honest enough to acknowledge that there is much we don't know. You may not be ready for the unknown, but you'd better be ready to adapt to it.

Chances are that life will deal us more unknown unknowns than known knowns and known unknowns. Change is rarely linear. When it comes to change, it's not just about wanting it. You've got to see it as the right move. You have to believe that change is in your best interest. But simply wanting change isn't enough; you've got to put in the work.

This is a good spot for me to address positivity. Positivity is not always your friend. Forced positivity can steer you away from reality. It's about balancing that optimism with a good dose of realism.

Your yellow brick road probably won't be a straight line. There will be twists and turns and potholes. You might even get lost, and your phone won't have a signal, GPS isn't working, and who has a map in their car in this day and age? How do you know which direction to take? There are so many options. We all want the "right" answer. What is the "correct" choice? What "should" I do?

Instead of searching for an absolute guarantee that doesn't exist (outside of death, taxes, or having to go to the bathroom five minutes into a road trip), reverse-engineer your path.

You may not fully see the future path, but you definitely see your past path. So review it:

What was the wrong answer?

What was the incorrect choice?

What should you not do again?

Sometimes your yellow brick road will lead you not *to* a faultless future but *away* from your perilous past. If you can accept that the changes you face in your life will most likely be nonlinear, you'll have a much easier time navigating them effectively.

I'm now going to take the opportunity to answer my own question:

**Why haven't you addressed your real problem yet?**

Let's look at the psychology of it. We survived as a species by being suspicious of things we're not familiar with. When we notice something is different, our brain thinks it might be dangerous. To change, we have to be aware of that animal instinct—to learn how to shut it down so we can step past our primal urge to maintain familiarity. Our brains and our egos love comfort and familiarity because comfort and familiarity keep us alive.

**Here are some examples of where ego could be at play for you in relation to a resistance to change:**

- **Your competence is being threatened.** If you're facing a change that questions or challenges your skills or knowledge, you might prefer to ignore the issue than admit that you don't know everything.
- **You're afraid of losing status.** Your ego might be strongly connected to your current level of authority. If you're facing an issue that could disrupt that position of power, you may dig in your heels and resist change.
- **You're comfortable with your identity.** If you're fighting to hold on to your identity—even (especially) at a subconscious level—it will be tough to change. If your ego is strongly connected to your current self-concept or way of doing things, anything threatening to change it will be met with resistance.
- **You're comfortable.** Period. Change means we have to step outside of our comfort zones, and it can be scary out there. The unknown can conjure up feelings of uncertainty and vulnerability, which are very scary for our egos because the ego needs predictability and stability to keep us alive.
- **You crave control.** Our egos like to be in the driver's seat so they can have control over situations in our lives.

Again, that's how they keep us alive. When we face change (especially change that is outside of our control) that we didn't ask for, our ego is amazing at keeping us safe by ensuring we stay exactly where we are.

Resistance to change can be seen as resistance to vulnerability and honesty. It's extremely uncomfortable and unsettling to think that the way you are operating—the way you've always operated—is no longer serving you.

Your ego sees vulnerability as an admission of failure and an acknowledgment that you aren't good enough. The fragility of ego clouds your vision of a better future, making every step toward it shorter or nonexistent.

**Not all resistance is effective resistance, though. What you may be protecting by resisting change, you are really projecting by assisting ego.**

Combine ego with the security of familiarity and the fear of the unknown, and you've got a powerful stay-stuck story. And remember—not all stories are rooted in fact.

Just like in Chapter 1, when I challenged you to get to the root of the real problem you're trying to solve, in this chapter, I want you to get good and clear on *the story behind your stuckness*.

You might be tempted to skip this step, but don't. You can only change if you're willing to do the work to find out why you haven't done it already.

By understanding what's keeping you stuck, you'll be in a good position to change or adapt to whatever change is happening (or will happen) around you.

In the following sections, I cover some other reasons you might be resisting change.

## Zero-Sum Bias

This is where you see change as win-lose, believing that you can't get what you want without someone else losing. "To bring myself up in life, I must bring others down." This bias is one of persistent pessimism and skepticism.

With the innovation of incredible technology such as self-driving cars and artificial intelligence (AI), zero-sum thinking has nearly 70% of Americans afraid of said self-driving cars and 52% feeling "more concerned than excited" about AI.

Progress, change, and innovation do not always need a negative outcome attached to the proposed positive. Yet, the zero-sum bias helps you validate your distaste for the new (even if the "new" is simply a better "old").

You are allowed to grow without it costing those around you. You are allowed to change course without losing. Change and failure do not have to be a dynamic duo like peanut butter and jelly.

## The Sunk-Cost Fallacy

The sunk-cost fallacy (aka irrational escalation) means continuing to forge ahead on a project, mission, or idea that's not working just because you've already invested significant time, money, and effort.

In 2003, 19-year-old Elizabeth Holmes founded Theranos, a tech company that aimed to revolutionize the health care industry with a new blood testing device. Walgreens saw a collaboration with Theranos as an opportunity to gain a strong competitive advantage, amping up their in-store health services while making them faster and more efficient.

However, red flags started popping up when people began questioning the reliability and accuracy of Theranos' blood-testing technology. Walgreens had invested so much time, effort, and resources implementing Theranos technology that they had a tough time walking away from the partnership. This is when the sunk cost fallacy started to grow.

Eventually, it came to light that Theranos had exaggerated its claims and misled its patients and investors. After Walgreens severed ties with Theranos, they were forced to settle a lawsuit brought forth by customers who received flawed blood test results—to the tune of $44M.

If you're in a situation where you're continuing on a path that isn't good for you, just because of the time, effort, or energy you've invested so far, take a look at it.

**Don't make decisions based on past costs. Make decisions based on future benefits.**

## Loss Aversion

Loss aversion describes what happens when we're more focused on how bad it would feel to lose than we are on how good it will feel to gain. This cognitive bias explains the tendency to prioritize avoiding losses over obtaining comparable or even better gains.

As human beings, we are more likely to avoid a loss than to seek a gain because of how our brains are wired. We fear losing something that is ours, whether it's a thought or a material object. And there's a psychological reason for that. (Of course there is.)

Three regions of the brain are activated in a situation involving loss aversion:

◆ **Amygdala:** Your amygdala is the part of your brain that's responsible for processing fear and creating a sense of anxiety when you sense danger. This part of your brain lights up when a spider lands on you and when you lose money. You experience a visceral reaction to danger and loss. That's because a cocktail of stress hormones such as adrenaline and cortisol are released throughout your body to give you energy and protect you from getting hurt. Your brain and body are programmed to be afraid of loss.

◆ **Striatum:** The striatum region of your brain is responsible for anticipating events and calculating prediction errors. Regardless of whether you're gaining or losing, the striatum is activated. But the striatum lights up more for losses than it does for gains.

◆ **Insular cortex:** The insular cortex reacts to disgust. Working with the amygdala, it helps us avoid certain types of behavior. Neuroscientists have discovered that the insular region of our brain lights up when we're experiencing loss. The higher we perceive a loss, the more activated the insula. This explains why we're disgusted by the thought of losing or missing out. (#fomo)

We have loss aversion to thank for prompting us to make decisions to avoid failure rather than to get us further ahead. (I'll go into this more in Chapter 3 when I talk about using the power of language to hack your brain.)

## The Ambiguity Effect

The pain we know is more comfortable than the pain we don't know (aka change). That's why the ambiguity effect can sneak up on us so often. The ambiguity effect is a bias that affects decision-making due to uncertainty or a lack of familiarity. New is scary, and old is safe. And with this mentality, innovation ceases to exist.

We can all think of examples of schools, governments, institutions, and companies that have held on to systems that aren't working instead of trying something new.

In the mid-1950s, the "king of rock," Elvis Presley, brought his never-before-seen blend of gospel, R&B, and country sound to the music scene with his now-famous dance moves. His performance and style were condemned as unusual and strange. It would not be the first or last time being innovative was mislabeled as unusual and strange. The ambiguity effect can cause us to mislabel unfamiliarity as bad.

Even if the path we're taking sucks, if we change things, we might be worse off than where we are now. Changing course means being brave enough to try something new in the hopes that you'll end up in a winning position.

## The Anchoring Effect

We can resist change if we've become so anchored to a specific plan that our perception is fixed. With the anchoring effect, we can believe so strongly in the current plan that our perception becomes distorted.

In a study conducted by Tversky and Kahneman (1974), high school students were asked to answer several math questions quickly. For example, students were asked to estimate the following in five seconds:

$$8 \times 7 \times 6 \times 5 \times 4 \times 3 \times 2 \times 1$$

Another group was given the same sequence in reverse:

$$1 \times 2 \times 3 \times 4 \times 5 \times 6 \times 7 \times 8$$

In the first case, the average guess was 2,250. In the second, the average estimate was 512. The correct answer to the problem is 40,320.

According to the researchers, the reason for this difference is that the students were trying to calculate the answer in their heads, and the group who had larger numbers to start with brought them to a larger starting point. They were *anchored* to a bigger number.

**Think about how the anchoring bias could be at work for you.**

Maybe you've committed to one career for your entire life but no longer feel fulfilled in that role. Maybe you've committed to a relationship that isn't what it used to be. Maybe you've committed to an internal dialogue that paints you as less-than or unworthy.

Remember, an anchor is meant to keep you stationary. Moments of stability are needed, but quality of life requires forward momentum. You must be willing to unanchor and anchor at different stages of your life.

"To reach Port, we must sail—sail, not tie at anchor—sail, not drift."

—*Franklin D. Roosevelt*

## Belief Perseverance

Have you ever clung to beliefs even when you had evidence that they might be wrong? If so, you may resist ditching those beliefs even if doing so would be in your best interest because you're so committed to them—like openly believing in Santa Claus in junior high (Savion 2009).

The reason for this is cognitive dissonance. Cognitive dissonance is a phenomenon that causes discomfort or stress due to conflicting beliefs. This psychological theory is at the root of most validation to stay stuck and continue down a path that doesn't serve us.

As human beings, we like to think that our beliefs are true and accurate. When information comes to the surface and challenges something we *know* to be true, we get very uncomfortable and enter a state of cognitive dissonance. Unfortunately, we often say that we "know" something to be true when we really mean that we aren't discerning between feeling like it's true, maintaining consistency even if wrong, and actual fact-based knowledge.

One good example of this would be saying that smoking helps you reduce stress. When you get stressed, you've built the habit of going out for a cigarette. You know very well that smoking is terrible for your health. But you rationalize that you only smoke when you're stressed or when there is a trigger. You continue to smoke, blaming stress and minimizing the known negative consequences, because you're just too stressed. To make this more bearable, you may ignore the correct information and hold on to your old beliefs to maintain internal consistency.

It's common for our beliefs to get so totally wrapped up with our identity that we feel like a failure if what we thought was true turns out to be false.

To protect you from pain, your ego will stop you from accepting new evidence so you can blissfully hold on to your self-esteem and do stuff that's not good for you. You may even look for carefully selected out-of-context research that makes it easier to defend your habits. This is belief perseverance requesting help from confirmation bias, where you only seek information that fits one idea—your idea.

In their book *Mistakes Were Made (But Not by Me)*, Dr. Carol Tavris and Dr. Elliot Aronson (2007) explain how the need to preserve our self-concept can lead to self-justification and a strengthening of our original beliefs. Much of what we know is simply what we've come to know through exposure, repetition, and acceptance of information.

Common beliefs that are entirely false include:

- Bubblegum takes a year to digest.
- Police are required to "protect and serve."
- We only use 10% of our brains.

- Blood is blue when depleted of oxygen.
- Napoleon was short.

These common beliefs are not true, yet you probably are second-guessing a few of them (I did, too, don't worry). When we're "sure" about our knowledge, we become "sure" about our thoughts, beliefs, and choices.

You will often defend your belief without fact-checking yourself if you believe you are right. Make sure you check your beliefs by asking yourself:

- Is there a possibility that I'm incorrect?
- Is there a possibility that things might have changed?
- Is there a possibility that I need to update this thought?

The killer of all progress is your self-justification for why you do things that merely hold you back in life. **Nothing is more harmful than unchecked conviction.** So let me ask you: Are you willing to change what's keeping you stuck?

As you can see from the list of reasons I just gave you, the majority of the time, it will be your own belief systems and hardwiring that are responsible for your position.

Consistency leads to progress unless you are consistently ineffective—then it just leads to staying stuck.

Taylor Swift has stayed relevant for two decades by doing her own version of her music, navigating and changing her approach as needed. Instead of losing the rights to her own music, she found a way to rerecord her songs to regain creative rights. The need to adapt parallels the need to change, and there's no doubt change can be hard. But it's much harder to stay stuck and hope for change than to identify the real issue and take the first few steps.

> "It might be hard for an egg to turn into a bird, but it would be a lot harder for a bird to learn how to fly while remaining an egg."
>
> —*C.S. Lewis*

So why haven't you changed your job, management team, relationship, bad habit, zip code?

"I don't know" isn't the answer you're looking for.

What's keeping you stuck? Are you honest enough with yourself to recognize what is keeping you stuck? If so, let's continue. If not, you're definitely not going to like this book.

**Lion:** I'd show him who was King of the Forest!

**All:** How?

**Lion:** How? Courage! What makes a King out of a slave?
Courage! What makes the flag on the mast to wave?
Courage! What makes the elephant charge his tusk
In the misty mist, or the dusky dusk? What makes the
muskrat guard his musk? Courage! What makes the
sphinx the seventh wonder? Courage! What makes
the dawn come up like thunder? Courage! What makes
the Hottentot so hot? What puts the "ape" in apricot?
What have they got that I ain't got?

**All:** Courage!

# CHAPTER 3

## The Power of Language

**KEY TASKS FROM THIS CHAPTER:**

- Check the things you believe to be true about yourself.
- Use neurolinguistic programming to change the way you talk about yourself.
- Reframe your situation to find the gain and not the loss around change.
- Find where you are on the Change Course Linguistic Matrix.

I opened Instagram the other day to David Goggins's wife recording him from her car. He was running an impromptu 100 miles in frigid weather, wearing nothing more than running shorts and a light hoodie. This took him over 12 hours, and there was no reason other than he felt like it.

If you don't know who David Goggins is, look him up. He's an extreme endurance athlete, a former Navy SEAL, and a best-selling author. He is the only man to complete SEAL training, US Army Ranger School, and Air Force Tactical Air Controller training, and he did so despite stress fractures, pneumonia, and sickle cell anemia. Oh, and he also had to lose over 100 pounds in three months at one point in his journey.

He's very blunt and very outspoken but rightfully so. He epitomizes grit and resilience and attributes his achievements to the power of self-talk and internal language.

Highlighting the significance of self-talk, Goggins is a prime example of how influential language can be when it comes to shaping your subconscious and achieving your own goals.

Recognizing when to change course and actually changing course are two different things. And here's where language and mindset come into play.

We often trap ourselves with our own narratives. The key is to break free from these patterns.

**You're not what you've done in the past; habits can always change.** And that's what change management is about—not just understanding change but also having the tools to navigate it effectively.

"Make sure your worst enemy doesn't live between your own two ears."

*—David Goggins*

"I'm bad with money."

"I can't get motivated."

"I have no willpower."

"I wish I could get it together."

"That person is so much more talented than I am. I'll never be good enough."

Language like this keeps you stuck. Ironically, language is also the simplest way to alter the course of your life and get unstuck.

**Show me your internal dialog, and I'll show you your future.**

Change your language. Change your life.

You become a prisoner of your past when you make absolute statements about your present condition and future potential based on things that have already happened.

This guarantees that your future state will be the same as your past and present.

**You must be willing to be wrong about the things you *think* you know.**

Companies that completely change course fascinate me. It is wild to think companies will spend millions of dollars on one intention, only to completely change course and become much more successful. Netflix was originally only meant to send DVDs in the mail. WD-40 was originally meant for aerospace use to protect the Atlas missile from rust (not for your rusty bicycle spokes). Gatorade was designed for athletes, and we know the $6.5 billion in sales comes primarily from nonathletes.

I decided to use the undoubtedly impressive AI tool ChatGPT to find more examples of companies that had a major pivot to success. ChatGPT is an artificial intelligence chatbot that uses a large language model to produce humanlike text responses. It even learns to craft its own response based on reinforcement learning from people's feedback.

To my surprise, YouTube was listed as a company that had pivoted significantly. ChatGPT said that YouTube started as a dating website before becoming the video library giant we all know and love today.

I was surprised that I hadn't heard that before! And I hadn't heard that before because it wasn't true. After the wonder and awe that my brain experienced, imagining such a massive course change on YouTube's part, I asked ChatGPT a follow-up question:

"Hey ChatGPT, is that actually true?"

I've never questioned AI before. I like to think I'm a pretty knowledgeable guy, but AI has been trained on a massive corpus of text, including books, websites, journals, and more, amounting to roughly 300 billion words.

And in this case, ChatGPT was wrong.

The AI chatbot apologized and explained that YouTube starting out as a dating website was a rumor that gained popularity, and it mistakenly reported it to me (and who knows how many other inquisitive minds) as fact.

Your brain is like a natural version of an AI in the sense that both are complex systems processing and generating language all the time.

**And your brain processes language misinformation as fact all the time.**

What lies are you holding onto as facts? And do you cherry-pick in favor of yourself or against yourself? Cherry-picking in favor of yourself would be believing you're a rock star and can do anything you want. Cherry-picking against yourself would be believing that you're the biggest loser ever and nobody sucks as bad as you. Lies contribute to self-fulfilling prophecies.

**"I never accomplish anything."**

Really? Never? Not even once? Rationalizing moments where you didn't accomplish something into an absolute statement is dishonest. And if you believe you never accomplish anything, you probably won't accomplish much because you believe that to be true.

Do you never accomplish anything because you don't give your full effort? Or do you never accomplish anything because you tell yourself you "never accomplish" anything as a current state, but in truth, you may not have yet accomplished everything you wanted in the past?

**Counterintuitively, we invest in strategies that keep us stuck.**

There's a true sense of confidence and a false sense of confidence. In both cases, it's about the repetition of thought, belief, and supporting action. People tend to get stuck in the action part. It goes like this:

"I'm confident that I suck because I never finish things."

You're confident of this because of your past action of not finishing things. But your past action of not finishing things is motivated by the belief that you never finish things because that's the language you allow to exist. If you can change the thought, you can change the action, which will change the outcome.

What if you chose the thought: "I will finish what I start." Believe that you will finish what you start. Commit to the actions required to eventually finish what you start. As a result, you'll finish what you start. Voilà! True confidence and proof of your ability.

Feelings are not facts. Just because you feel that you never finish things doesn't mean it's true. Your history does not indicate your ability. Stop using incorrect language to lie to yourself.

Language based in truth or fact gives you a chance to change. Language based in lies or feelings gives you a reason to stay stuck.

**"I'm not good at anything."**

Is that really true? You can't think of *one* thing you're good at? Like parking, or making popcorn, or playing video games? It is *not true* that you're "not good at anything." You're just discounting what you *are* good at and embellishing what you aren't good at.

Michael Jordan was cut from his high school basketball team for being too short and not good enough. He had the opportunity to tell himself that he wasn't good at anything. He had the opportunity to tell himself that he wasn't good at basketball. Instead, he took the inevitable disappointment of not making the team as an opportunity to improve his craft. He consistently put in the work to ensure a moment of not being good enough was just a moment rather than an identity.

I have a rule for anyone I work with, from executives to students: You can't say you aren't good at something if you haven't put in the time and effort required to be good at it. This goes for any negative label statement that can be removed by action. Action follows language, so if the language you are using is a lie or half-truth even, you will be left acting out that lie.

> "The great enemy of truth is very often not the lie—deliberate, contrived and dishonest—but the myth—persistent, persuasive and unrealistic. ... We subject all facts to a prefabricated set of interpretations. We enjoy the comfort of opinion without the discomfort of thought."
>
> —*John F. Kennedy (1962)*

The half-truths and subtle but persistent myths that creep into your narratives and language patterns influence who you are and, consequently, who you become. When you believe something to be absolutely true without even thinking about it, that's just conditioning. It's language.

Just as AI tools use language learning, our minds process and generate language based on our experiences, knowledge, and understanding of the world. Language matters in making sure we're honest with ourselves and our self-talk, because the wrong language inputs can create the wrong language outputs—which leads us to make those decisions that negatively affect us.

This is particularly relevant in the context of ChatGPT, which, like our brains, relies on its training data to generate responses. If the input data contains biases or inaccuracies, both ChatGPT and your brain may generate responses that reflect those issues.

That means that even when you are dishonest about your current ability to be better (true), you reinforce past habits that say you are a poor performer (not true). This is like saying you'll never learn how to ride a bike, so you won't take the training wheels off.

What language inputs are hurting your progress? Start paying attention to what you say to yourself and about yourself throughout your day. At work or at home, whether you are working on a goal or catch a glimpse of yourself in the mirror, spot the language that's being used in both positive and negative experiences.

**Who you have been is not who you have to be forever.**

We have just as much power to say, "I haven't learned how to ride a bike yet, but I know I can commit more to trying." We can look at ourselves in the mirror and say, "I may have been scared in the past, but that doesn't mean I have to let fear stop me from moving forward."

It's important to recognize that getting stuck is a normal part of life. Staying stuck is not.

## Chronic versus Acute Stuckness

At the height of my powerlifting career, I was unstoppable. I had reached my ultimate goal of deadlifting seven plates (per side), or 675 pounds. As an amputee and type 1 diabetic, I never thought I'd be able to lift that amount of weight.

The world was not designed for a one-handed guy like myself. I struggled to find machines I could use. I struggled to learn how to lift weights safely. Most of all, I struggled with being stuck in a situation I didn't want and not getting the results I wished for.

I never accepted my stuckness, though. I adapted to my environment and found ways to lift weights (even if they were unconventional). Whenever I felt stuck again, I addressed where I was stuck, why, and what I could do to get unstuck.

The answers are rarely difficult yet sometimes require creativity and commitment.

I'll never forget being temporarily stuck at 500 pounds as the hook I used to lift with my residual limb kept sliding off.

"This is never going to work."

"I won't be able to lift heavier."

"I'm not going to reach my goals like this."

Easy thoughts to have when you're acutely stuck. I just knew there had to be a way. There's always a way.

So, one day I took my wrist wrap from my gym bag and thought, "What if I wrapped this around the lifting hook to create more contact force?"

It looked silly. And no one used it like I was trying to use it. But what could it hurt to try?

That healthy questioning of my stuckness resulted in a powerlifting career and story that catapulted me to notoriety in the fitness industry.

Acute stuckness is normal. It happens, and it's supposed to happen. Like a great video game or any hero's journey, there are always multiple points of conflict while progressing. If you want zero conflict, you opt for zero progress.

Chronic stuckness, on the other hand, is natural. Lack of progress gets you stuck. Ineffective self-talk keeps you stuck. The life of a chronically stuck person is not always terrible, though. It's not what they want at all, but it's also not bad enough to change. The willingness to initiate change isn't quite there. Language perpetuates beliefs. Beliefs perpetuate biases. And both serve to keep that stuck feeling in life consistent with the actions you take.

It is unnatural to resist progress and adaptation.

Chronic stuckness exists by choice or lack of choice and is heavily influenced by a self-deprecating inner dialogue or inner language.

## Internal Language

Internal language plays a significant role in effective change management. Self-talk and cognitive restructuring techniques emphasize the power of transforming negative self-talk into positive and adaptive thoughts.

Our internal dialogue directly affects our brain activity and decision-making processes. Yet, people disregard the importance of language. Doing so is like building a house on an unstable foundation.

In the *Dhammapada,* the Buddha remarked, "We are shaped by our thoughts, and we become what we think." Both Chinese folklore and Buddhist texts refer to the "monkey mind," or the constant state of restless, unsettled, and chaotic thoughts most of us endure.

You're probably familiar with the monkey mind. You go about your day and find yourself excessively ruminating on your lack of success in the past, present, or future, cutting yourself down with negative thoughts, and overwhelming yourself into a state of paralysis—all while taking your lunch break in silence.

You spend more time with yourself than anyone else in the world, and there is a mountain of research that shows how much internal narrative and dialogue affect our thoughts, beliefs, and decisions. And monkey brain is a pretty real thing.

Monkey brain can accurately be referred to as your "default mode network," which is simply a part of your brain that controls self-rumination passively. Self-rumination or self-thought can be good or bad while examining the past, present, or future.

Think of the default mode network as a backstage crew orchestrating your mental narratives when you aren't actively engaged in external tasks. If you find yourself talking negatively about your looks, performance, or current position in life compared to where you "should be," that's the default mode network at work.

Unfortunately, some people experience more negative self-referential language than others, especially people with depression, where rumination is preferential to negative remarks (Hsu et al. 2021). If you consistently train your brain to see limitations and negatives, the passive rumination that happens throughout the day is more likely to favor pessimism.

In one of my change management keynotes, I handed out those old-school cheap 3D glasses to everyone in the audience. You know, the ones made of thin cardboard that have one blue lens and one red lens. Once they put them on, I start showing objects in different colors and shades, asking them to shout out the color. Due to the glasses, the colors were distorted, so they mostly said blue or red. I do this to show the effect that biases, mental health states, and language have on our view of everything in the world.

Preference is often given to negative rumination or thoughts when you experience disruptive change and feeling stuck. That preference is similar to the 3D glasses skewing your perception, and if you aren't careful, that lens can be mistaken for reality, a reality that embraces staying stuck.

Feeling stuck increases the vulnerability of the default mode network to reinforce negative feelings with thoughts, resulting in this cognitive-emotive negative feedback loop:

You feel stuck.

You get frustrated.

Prolonged frustration leads to depressive episodes.

You follow with negative self-talk and disempowering language.

You stay stuck.

Neuroscientists have used MRI and EEG technologies to study correlations between neural activity and self-talk (Moser et al. 2017). The language we use internally affects brain function and structure.

Let me repeat that:

**The language we use internally affects brain function and structure.**

As you repeat habits and thoughts, your brain forms and strengthens neural pathways that are like grooves in your brain. With repetition, these pathways strengthen and become second nature. Bad habits such as harmful and dishonest internal dialogs and self-talk wire the brain to repeat the damaging behaviors.

Your brain has this incredible ability to restructure, reorganize, and rewire new neural pathways through internal and external inputs, though. This process, called *neuroplasticity,* allows you to quite literally change your brain structure simply through the repetition of new habits and the weakening of old habits.

This self-directed neuroplasticity is possible through repetition, practice, filtering out unwanted thoughts, and replacing them with effective ones. Unwanted behaviors can be traced back to maladaptive pathways that contribute to feeling hopeless and self-deprecating.

Here's an example of how language can work against you: I've had clients desperate for change who tell me they've tried everything. I'll say, "Oh really? What have you tried?"

Then they list three things. And of those three things, they say they gave each a 6/10 effort. Google shows 295 million results for "best diets," so they were nowhere near trying everything. It's amazing how "everything" can be so limited. Because they've wired their brains to believe the word "everything" means "a few things," they are left feeling hopeless. I would feel hopeless, too, if I had given 100% of my effort and tried everything possible.

It always goes back to linguistics and language. Consistently telling yourself that little lie about having tried everything fortifies a false belief. We complain about our discomfort but fail to take action to change the language, let alone the habit and action.

Neuroplasticity is proof that change is possible. Rewiring your brain for change requires repetition to strengthen the new pathway until it's automatic and weaken the old pathway until it's gone.

But why is this important for you? You didn't reach for this book to reshape your brain—you want to manage this change and get unstuck.

**Your brain is willing and able to change in whatever direction you start pointing it in.**

And if you accept your monkey brain's language inputs without review—especially during volatile moments in your life or organization—you can't expect trustworthy thoughts.

The damning self-talk that has kept you stuck can be changed if you're willing to start focusing on what you can control: your language. If you grant yourself permission to start talking to yourself differently, a whole new world of possibilities opens up for you.

A great way to start making this shift is by trying the neuro-linguistic programming technique of changing your phrasing around habits from the present tense ("I always mess everything up") to past tense ("I may have messed up in the past, but I'm not my past patterns, and I will improve daily").

By reframing the person you are—from being defined by habits of your past to who you used to be—you can isolate bad habits or patterns to the past. This gives you a chance to think and act differently. By applying a habit of your past to your current self, you are setting up your current and future self to become a carbon copy of the past, dictating that how you've "always been" is how you will always be—but that's a choice.

**Here's how it looks in action:**

I'm a lazy person. → I have been lazy in the past, but that's not who I am.

I'm a procrastinator. → I have procrastinated in the past, but that's not who I am.

I'm a failure. → I have failed in the past, but that's not who I am.

I'm a quitter. → I have quit on myself in the past, but that's not who I am.

**Here's a formula to use for whatever you're lying to yourself about:**

Just because [BAD EVENT] doesn't mean I can't [GOAL] as long as I stop [BAD HABIT] and start [IMPROVED HABIT].

Here's an example:

Just because I was born with a disability doesn't mean I can't be confident in my body as long as I stop telling myself I'm broken and start embracing who I am.

The language you choose to use, whether actively or passively, reinforces your beliefs and subsequent actions.

Another language hack you can try is related to the topic of loss aversion (see Chapter 2). Phrasing a question as a loss may increase loss aversion, while phrasing that same question as a gain may reduce loss aversion, creating a more optimal outcome.

When facing change, whether expected or unexpected, try framing the options to highlight the potential gain for you rather than the loss.

Let's look at Netflix as an example. Netflix sent out more than 5 billion DVDs by mail, which was their entire claim to fame. In late 2023, they sent out their last DVD. It would be easy to say Netflix lost that part of their business. But by using a "gain frame," Netflix can now focus on improving its streaming platform and innovate forward because it no longer has to send 4,500 DVDs an hour (or overload the US Postal Service with more than one million disc returns per day).

When you start thinking better, life starts improving because you have the upper hand over the one thing you can control: yourself.

Remember, you can always change your circumstances, even if that just means changing your narrative.

Once you decide to get the upper hand over the thoughts, beliefs, and actions that keep you stuck, you realize that most of your pain comes only from yourself and that quality of life is achieved through internal thoughts, not external circumstances.

## The Change Course Linguistic Matrix

For years I found myself needing to learn more and do more instead of ever actually doing something. Why be productive when I didn't know enough to be perfect?

Honestly? I wanted to be better than better. I needed to know everything before I started.

I fell in love with videography six years ago and content creation in general. I just needed to get a camera.

Once I got a camera, I saw that there were better cameras than my camera, so I was already losing. Then I needed a better lens to get the perfect shot.

Once I finally got that lens, I realized I was missing the fancy lights and microphones, that my walls weren't sound-proof, and that I had to buy a few different software programs to compete with the pros. Then I needed to learn color theory and the rules for all things film and photo. I was just starting out, but in reality, I didn't start for a long time after getting all the equipment.

I was so far behind from the best of the best, and that "need" for perfectionism had me telling myself, "I just need [insert excuse here]. Then I'll get started."

It took me four years to actually start shooting video regularly. And it was only when I stopped making excuses about why I wasn't shooting that I started to get better. I told myself everything I wanted to hear to avoid the pains of being terrible when you start doing something unfamiliar and new.

Our maladaptive avoidance mechanisms such as procrastination, self-deprecating narratives, and ineffective language patterns dampen action. Now there are times when competency and external resources are required—I have no linguistic models that will replace the need for a chainsaw if you need to cut down a tree, and I can't motivate you enough to cut random wires in your wall to replace the competency an electrician has. Skills can and should be learned, but the need to learn more does not remove the responsibility of the work you need to do that is in your wheelhouse.

People have varying levels of competency and language efficacies in different areas of their lives. And as I discuss in the

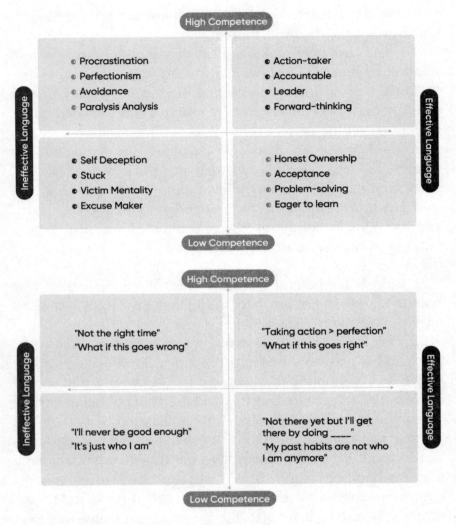

Figure 3.1 The Linguistic Matrix for Change.

next chapter, it's crucial that you see where you are in order to face it and fix what needs to be fixed.

I developed the Linguistic Matrix for Change (see Figure 3.1) to determine where you are, with the ultimate goal being to get you to the quadrant at the upper right.

## QUADRANT 1: KNOW IT ALL; DO IT NAUGHT

My natural default quadrant lives here. I want to be perfect so badly that it often leads to avoidance and procrastination. In pursuing perfectionism, you learn all the information you need to start.

You know enough to act. Yet, you still procrastinate.

Perfectionism is just procrastination dressed in gold.

In this model, ineffective language attempts to validate your paralysis:

"It's not the right time."

"What if it goes wrong?"

"What if I don't know enough?"

Chances are, you already have all the tools you need to tackle your current struggles head-on. People in this quadrant need to examine a little less and act more.

Combat ineffective language with effective language such as:

"What if this goes right?"

"What if now is as good a time as any?"

"What if I know enough already?"

This language will help shift you out of the stuck category and into action.

## QUADRANT 2: CHANGE MAKER

This quadrant is the ultimate goal of anyone looking to get unstuck, stay unstuck, and manage change. Here, you balance effective language with the proper skills to commit to action. You operate with urgency to act but grace to make mistakes. You hold yourself accountable and are able to lead others to this quadrant as well.

More often than not, people who change their world—and the world at large—exist here. When change happens externally or needs to happen internally, you get to the root of the problem. You ask, "What is the real issue here that I might be avoiding?" No matter the size of the problem, people in this quadrant take a "How can I . . ." approach to adapt.

Extreme ownership, accountability, and living by example indicate you operate in this quadrant. Blame and certainty don't really exist here. Change makers celebrate their small, consistent wins and stack more effective habits as they go, embodying the definition of a role model.

Set your sights on becoming a change maker.

## QUADRANT 3: THE STUCK

This is a rough place to be. You haven't begun to explore the options or tools you need or might even have already. Everything in life seems to be happening *to* you, and it feels like the world hates you. The ineffective language runs rampant here, accepting limiting beliefs such as, "I'll never be good enough" and "I'm just not destined for anything good." These linguistic fables about who you are and your potential are not facts—they're just strong feelings that anyone who is stuck can experience.

If you find yourself here, you must start shifting your language to more effective models and fact-checking your thoughts. Just because it has been rough doesn't mean it has to stay like that. You don't have to continue to be who you have been.

Don't allow your language to fortify a future you don't want for yourself. You are a victim of nothing. You are worthy of your own effort. Your first effort can be acknowledging, "I may not like where I am right now, but I'm willing to change that, starting by removing limiting beliefs about myself."

## QUADRANT 4: ALMOST THERE

Arguably the easiest way out of any struggle is to align effective language with a plan to succeed. You may not know exactly what you need to do, but that's okay. Maybe you need to get more schooling or self-education. Maybe you are acquiring the tools as you go.

The person in this quadrant recognizes that they're getting close. They choose to use effective language to keep themselves motivated and focus on solving problems with their narratives (not creating them). They live in a state of acceptance and welcome the learning curve that comes with time, effort, and an effective mindset.

The Linguistic Matrix for Change can help you pinpoint where you are in your journey to get unstuck and change course as needed without creating your own rough seas to further complicate the journey.

Trust yourself, weigh out options, and understand that change is a normal part of life.

The good news is that we are biologically wired to adapt.

The quality of your life depends on the quality of your thoughts.

So why do we get stuck in negative spirals, convincing ourselves that we have to endure situations we hate?

Changing your perspective and how you talk about yourself and your problems can improve all areas of your life.

Consider this story:

A wealthy man was tired of hearing his son complain that he worked too much. So the man took his son on a trip to an underdeveloped country to show his boy how lucky he was.

They stayed on a farm with people who lived in poverty. The man made sure they ate dinner with the family every night to show the boy how good they had it at home.

After the trip, the father smugly asked the boy, "Did you enjoy the trip, seeing how poor people live?"

The boy somberly replied, "I did, Father. I saw that poor people have more dogs than us and instead of fancy lanterns, they have the night sky. I saw that instead of a nice pool they have an endless river that everyone is welcome to. I saw that instead of a tall, cold metal fence, they have an open house and trust their neighbors. I saw that poor people have dinner with each other every night and love each other endlessly."

The father could barely collect himself before his boy said, "I wish we were poor, Father."

**Your perspective is your prerogative.**

Don't become a victim of your perspective. Don't dwell on what you lack. Practicing negativity is easy and natural, but it's not productive. There are no rewards for hardship in life.

Facing change can be challenging, but staying in a negative cycle is worse. Clarity in calamity is essential. Accepting misery might feel easier, but action is needed to break free from it.

The characters in *The Wonderful Wizard of Oz* were constantly reinforcing their pain through their language and self-talk. The Scarecrow was convinced he didn't have a brain, but he was able to think. The Tin Man told himself he didn't have a heart, but he was able to love. The Lion told himself he was a coward, but he was brave.

Language shapes your reality. Absolute statements about our condition and potential based on past experiences limit us. We can change the narrative and open up new possibilities. Change starts with recognizing and addressing the problem and altering our internal dialogue to facilitate a shift in perspective and action.

Remember, we know for sure that our internal dialogue directly affects brain activity. The way we talk to ourselves affects our neural pathways, emotional regulation, and decision-making processes (Brinthaupt and Morin 2023; Gibson and Foster 2007).

So use the power of language to support you on your journey.

**Fiction creates friction. Detangle the assumptions and feelings from the facts so you can change with less resistance and more effective habits.**

| | |
|---|---|
| **Lion:** | Wait a minute, fellahs. I was just thinkin'. I really don't want to see the Wizard this much. I better wait for you outside. |
| **Scarecrow:** | What's the matter? |
| **Tin Man:** | Oh, he's just scared again. |
| **Dorothy:** | Don't you know the Wizard's going to give you some courage? |
| **Lion:** | I'd be too scared to ask him for it. |
| **Dorothy:** | Oh, well, then—we'll ask him for you. |
| **Lion:** | I'd sooner wait outside. |
| **Dorothy:** | But why? Why? |
| **Lion:** | Because I'm still scared! |

# CHAPTER 4

# Prescription to Change

**KEY TASKS FROM THIS CHAPTER:**

- ◆ Give yourself permission to change from who you were to who you can be.
- ◆ Give yourself a prescription to change to act on that permission.
- ◆ Spot competing commitments that might hold you back, and compare the benefits of the new change to the old commitments.

I hate participating in the adversity Olympics to see who has it worse, but it's important to acknowledge what people have to deal with.

My family had very little money. I vaguely remember wondering why we went to church to get Cookie Crisp cereal and canned food. I wondered why my parents were so stressed about buying things. I really wondered why my bedroom door was literally a piece of wood with a hole where the door knob should be.

My entire life, my family struggled to get by. And on top of that, I had a disability that painted me as unarguably different. So I leaned into that difference.

I had huge aspirations for fitness businesses and companies, but they weren't just dreams. They were such strong aspirations that I could taste them. I busted my tail trying to create the financially secure life I dreamed of.

Unfortunately, no matter how hard I worked, I found myself broke and struggling for years. It got so bad that I was ready to give up. Many times.

My brother, who fought hard to make something of himself, ended up with severe credit card debt in college, inevitably leading him to leave pharmacy school. His dream was shattered. But later he applied to pharmacy school again and even went on to earn a master's degree. He earned the highest education and became the highest earner in our family.

I always looked up to him and, at that time, more than ever. He was the only person in my life who didn't let me quit. The irony of my pharmacist brother giving me my prescription to change is not lost on me: "You really want to do this? You can live with me. I won't charge you because you can barely afford life, but you can't afford to give up that dream," he said, giving me permission to change.

People will always be waiting in the wings, telling us that we should change something in our lives. That's great and all, but it often isn't enough to motivate us. It's easy to give ourselves permission to stay stuck, saying things such as, "It's not the right time. I'll wait it out a bit and see if things get easier." If that's you, take this book as a sign that right now is the right time.

To start making moves toward who you want to be, you need to give yourself permission to change the way you've always done and thought about things.

**It's time to help your future self by getting rid of your past self and being your best self right now.**

That is what's going to happen when you give yourself permission to move through these three phases:

◆ Making your problems public to yourself (subconscious → conscious)

◆ Sharing them with those closest to you (conscious → communicated)

◆ Broadcasting them to the world (communicated → broadcast)

**With your future self hanging in the balance, will you give yourself permission to start modeling the habits of your best self?**

Giving yourself permission to change is a crucial step in the process of actualizing personal transformation.

Tony Robbins says that the biggest resource we have is being resourceful. You don't have to be Tony Robbins to know that your power to change lies in your power to solve problems—first in your own mind and then in tangible ways.

If you fall into quicksand, you probably aren't going to shrug and let yourself sink. You'll yell for help or try to find a branch or something to get yourself out of that scenario. You don't need someone to say, "Hey, dude, you probably shouldn't be in quicksand right now."

If something is happening in your life that you're not happy about, focus on what you can control, not what you can't. Then give yourself permission to do something about it.

The good news is that you have personal agency. When you decide that it's time to change and that you're capable of making this change, you're halfway there. No more being a passive bystander in your life. This takes you from a fixed mindset (which leads to resistance to change) to a growth mindset (where you embrace change as an opportunity for growth).

Sometimes giving yourself permission to change is the catalyst you need to act. It's like giving yourself the mental green light to change your behavior.

Giving yourself permission to change is active. Giving yourself permission to stay stuck is passive.

We give ourselves permission to stay stuck by not being honest with ourselves about what it's doing to us. We're not honest with ourselves at all about the consequences of staying the same. Yet, we give ourselves permission to stay stuck by saying we'll do something eventually or using language that tricks us into being passive.

But why in the world would you give yourself permission to stay stuck?

I mean, look what happened to King Louis XVI. As head of the French monarchy in 1774 at the pinnacle of a 1,000-year dynasty, King Louis XVI had total and absolute power.

Aristocracy is great when you're one of the aristocrats. But everyone else suffers. No matter how much his subjects hated him and his antiquated hierarchy, it didn't matter because he was in charge. His privilege was more important than his subjects' suffering.

Living in the lap of luxury just as his royal family had before him, Louis stubbornly and selfishly avoided fixing the economic and civil unrest and disparities. But because of centuries of extravagant spending and investing in things such as the American Revolution, there wasn't a lot in the purse for the peasants.

While his subjects were basically starving to death, King Louis XVI was throwing masquerades and balls with extravagant feasts. A slap in the face to those suffering.

As the years passed, Louis's people become more discontent. Ultimately, the common folks formed an assembly to rise up against him and the French monarchy. The French Revolution ensued, and King Louis XVI fled the country. He was later arrested and charged with treason in 1792. The monarchy was abolished after a millennium-long reign, and a year later, Louis was put to death.

Sometimes, the inability to adapt to new circumstances or change can result in societal stagnation, civil unrest, and, in extreme cases such as that of the French monarchy, the downfall of entire empires and a trip to the guillotine.

In this book, I discuss a range of different psychological barriers to change (fear, cognitive dissonance, ego, control, and so on). Permission to stay stuck tends to revolve around your competing commitments that reside in the floorboards of your mind.

Competing commitments are conflicting goals or desires that you might hold, often unconsciously, that can thwart your ability to achieve your desired change.

It's natural (and comfortable) to want to maintain familiarity. But when a change is truly desired or required, these competing commitments are threats to both implementing and sustaining change (Table 4.1).

Men's health, news coverage, podcasts, viral social media posts—everything about my life between 2012 and 2019 revolved around fitness. I was known as the "one-handed powerlifter," and I loved it. Until I was ready to pivot.

**Table 4.1** Competing Goal Analysis

| Goal | Competing commitment | Result |
|---|---|---|
| Weight loss | Eat snacks and be sedentary | No change |
| Get a promotion | Maintain current workload and processes<br>Fear of more responsibility | No change |
| Innovative company | Maintain traditional process<br>Fear of unknown | No change |
| Meet someone new | Homebody and antisocial<br>Fear of embarrassing yourself | No change |
| Start new hobby | Spend all time doing old hobby<br>Fear of sucking at it | No change |
| Quit drinking | Hang out at bars with friends<br>Fear of not being accepted | No change |
| Build online business | Can't stop watching cat videos<br>Fear of being too busy for cat videos | No change |

I wanted to be more than the disabled fitness guy. I wanted to be recognized for thought leadership and speaking on change management. I really wanted to change course. But I also didn't want to lose the popularity and name I had built after so many years.

My competing commitment was to remain that disabled fitness guy while somehow evolving into the speaker I have fortunately become today. Essentially, I was pushing a door that needed to be pulled and wondering why it didn't open (don't lie, you've done it, too).

"What if it doesn't work?"

"It sounds nice ... Maybe later."

"People will think you're dumb."

"No one is going to want to hire you."

"What if you lose the results of all that hard work you did?"

My competing commitments were quiet, but my fears of them were loud.

I had to give myself permission to make mistakes.

I had to give myself permission to do it, scared.

I had to give myself permission to act.

To give yourself permission to change means to take ownership of the current situation, what you've done in the past, and what you have to do differently moving forward.

It's acknowledging a less-than-desirable situation and giving yourself permission to adapt to your surroundings. If someone wants to come over to my house, that's great, but they need permission.

Similar to vampire folklore requiring they be invited into your home to come in, change requires your invitation. The real vampire here is not change. It's the resistance to change. Most of us are sitting there looking at the door and hoping change happens, but we hesitate to invite it in. That is a problem that needs your permission to be solved.

Let's look at a few examples of how this might play out.

## Scenario 1: Job Dissatisfaction

Sarah is an upbeat marketing professional who is incredible at her job. Unfortunately for Sarah and many people like her, she feels unfulfilled and devalued. She desires a career shift. She wants to work in health care but is afraid of having to "start over" and the societal expectations that come with having a great job with benefits and a pension.

### PERMISSION TO CHANGE

Sarah gives herself permission to bypass the stigma and fears of what people might think so that she can explore new career paths. She acknowledges her right to pursue fulfillment and grants herself the freedom to take steps toward a health care career. Sarah understands that changing course is not a sign of failure but rather a sign of adaptation—a skill set that has kept the human species alive. Good for you, Sarah!

Humans are given multiple tools to stay alive, and they all "work." But to let our animalistic survival brain dictate that all unfamiliarity is dangerous is a tad bit dramatic; learning a new skill (while still maintaining her old skill) is hardly a brush with death.

### PRESCRIPTION TO CHANGE

Sarah tasks herself with transforming ideas to action. She starts researching how to get into health care, looks for possible roles and what responsibilities they would entail, and what she would need in terms of schooling. She weighs the pros and cons according to her desired career and assesses what needs to change to allow her to course-correct, financially and time-wise.

### BENEFITS FROM CHANGE

- **Increased confidence:** By allowing herself to consider a change, Sarah gains confidence in her decision-making skills and feels more empowered.
- **Reduced anxiety:** Giving herself permission eases Sarah's anxiety about stepping away from her current career, allowing her to embrace change positively.
- **Increased fulfillment:** Sarah is positioning herself to feel more fulfilled in her career, where she will spend 25% of her time.

## Scenario 2: Relationship Dynamics

Mark has faithfully committed to loving someone who treats him poorly. He feels stuck in a toxic relationship and fears judgment from friends and family if he chooses to leave. He struggles with guilt, lack of romantic fulfillment, and maintaining societal expectations.

## PERMISSION TO CHANGE

Mark gives himself permission to prioritize his well-being and happiness. He acknowledges that he deserves a healthy and fulfilling relationship, even if it means making difficult choices because he recognizes that love is not enough when you also need effort, respect, and growth.

## PRESCRIPTION TO CHANGE

Mark goes to therapy, sets boundaries, and eventually decides to end his toxic relationship, prioritizing not only his mental health but also the happiness he gave up for so long.

## BENEFITS FROM CHANGE

- **Emotional relief:** Granting himself permission helps alleviate guilt and internal conflict, allowing Mark to focus on self-care and healing.
- **Increased assertiveness:** Mark becomes more assertive in future relationships, recognizing the importance of setting boundaries and prioritizing his own needs along with the needs of others.
- **Increased fulfillment:** By setting boundaries and establishing his worth, Mark's next relationship will bring him more of what he truly wants, not just what he tolerates. Mark is now positioned to find fulfillment in himself and his next partner.

## Scenario 3: Health and Lifestyle Change

Alex struggles with obesity but feels overwhelmed by societal standards and self-doubt. He lacks confidence to commit to a healthier lifestyle and isn't sure what to do to reach his goals.

## PERMISSION TO CHANGE

Alex gives himself permission to prioritize his health and well-being. He acknowledges that he deserves to lead a healthier life, regardless of external pressures but rather for himself.

## PRESCRIPTION TO CHANGE

Alex begins exercising regularly, at first by walking, then progressing to body weight workouts at home, and then eventually joining a gym as his comfort increases. He adopts a balanced diet rather than a fast-food diet, feeling more motivated and committed to his health goals.

## BENEFITS FROM CHANGE

- **Improved self-esteem:** By granting himself permission, Alex's self-esteem improves, and he becomes more comfortable getting support from a dietitian and fitness coach.
- **Embracing change:** With self-permission, Alex navigates setbacks appropriately, understanding that change is not a linear process or an overnight transformation.
- **Increased fulfillment:** Alex's fulfillment grows every day as he starts to believe in himself and his ability to take actions in the right direction. Every meal and every step is a win, and the compound effect of those daily wins will inevitably pay off.

Both in your professional and your personal life, you must be willing to let go of how things used to be so that you can give yourself permission to change.

This is the precursor, the catalyst to change: the decision to do it. I've accepted where I currently am and want to change. While some changes require less urgency than others, no change has to be dramatic.

Aside from the must-do's to stay alive, you likely won't change 20 years of habits all at once. The same way you won't lose 20 pounds all at once.

**It takes repeated micro-steps to change course.**

Making continuous decisions in the right direction while limiting decisions in the wrong direction doesn't merely direct you to the best course—it *is* the best course.

That's what I'll talk about next.

**Leader:**    She's ... she's ... dead! You've killed her!
**Dorothy:**   I—I didn't mean to kill her ... really I didn't!
               It's ... it's just that he was on fire!
**Leader:**    Hail to Dorothy! The Wicked Witch is dead!
**Dorothy:**   You mean, you're ... you're all happy about it?
**Leader:**    Very happy—now she won't be able to hit us with
               a broom anymore!

# CHAPTER 5

# See It, Face It, Fix It

**KEY TASKS FROM THIS CHAPTER:**

◆ Use the "See It, Face It, Fix It" tool to tackle all obstacles in life with urgency and effectiveness.
◆ Recognize problems with honesty and ownership.
◆ Face each problem from a standpoint of what you can do from here instead of what you could have done in the past.
◆ Take action to progress toward a future you want and away from a past you don't want.

In Dr. Spencer Johnson's timeless classic *Who Moved My Cheese?* (1998), four rats are in a maze with cheese that suddenly moves from its familiar location. While the main story seems to focus on two of the characters, Hem and Haw, as they resist and avoid finding new cheese until one slowly ventures out, the other two characters, Sniff and Scurry, go about change differently. As soon as the cheese moves, they notice and immediately go in search of the cheese. Toward the end of the book, Haw finally works up the courage to find new cheese and sees that Sniff and Scurry are way ahead of him and have even found more cheese in different places. There is no overanalysis or avoidance on their part, just a quick reaction to change with a big payoff: new cheese.

Think about a time when you had a negative thought about yourself. A time where you caught yourself thinking a losing thought such as, "I'm not worth it," "Nobody will ever date me," "I'll never get a better job than this," etc.

Got one? Okay. Hold it for a minute.

When I was younger, I battled losing thoughts all day, every day. When I woke up in the morning, my first thought was a losing one: "How will I hide my hand today?"

As I mentioned back in Chapter 3, there's a lot of noise in our heads, and that's okay. Welcome to being human. But your job is to determine which of your thoughts will help you and which will hurt you. This takes work, and it is an ongoing process, but it is possible to do. The "See It, Face It, Fix It" process will help.

**You can't fix what you're not willing to face.** And you can't face something you don't see. It's that simple.

Consider this story:

An ancient king grew tired of his noblemen and people constantly complaining about the state of affairs in his kingdom. He decided to test the resolve of his people by placing a heavy, oddly shaped boulder in the middle of a path known to be the fastest route in and out of the city.

The king was curious to see how the noblemen and wealthy folks might move the boulder as this was the most efficient route to take. To his surprise, the wealthiest, strongest, and smartest men turned their backs to the boulder, often giving up before attempting to move it or giving it a slight push only to retreat back the way they came.

The king was confused about how little effort these noblemen exerted and how easily they took the longer, harder route.

Just before the king left, he saw a peasant approach the boulder. The poor man with nothing but a knapsack to his name pushed and pushed and pushed on the boulder with all his might. The king was tempted to intervene but noticed the peasant wandered off into the forest. He quickly returned with a few fallen tree trunks and created a lever system to move the boulder successfully.

The proud peasant almost walked away until he noticed a purse under the boulder. Much to his surprise, the purse was filled with gold coins along with a note from the king, which said, "To the person who faces the obstacle on their intended path, the spoils are worth the struggle."

The peasant in this example used a technique that Sniff, Scurry, and even Dorothy used to make it through their disruptive changes.

"See It, Face It, Fix It" is the Swiss Army knife for problem-solving and the foundation on which the Changing Course process you're about to learn is built.

I want you to get familiar with "See It, Face It, Fix It," not only because you'll be taking it with you to problem-solve as you go through the next three chapters of this book but also so you can use it long after you finish reading it. It's a tool that requires clarity, honesty, and responsibility. But it's effective in any problem-solving scenario.

In the story above, the peasant saw the boulder and knew he had to find a way around it to continue on his journey (See It). He then discovered that he was not strong enough to move the boulder without some assistance (Face It). Finally, he built some tools to help him get it out of his way (Fix It).

The majority of people live in a state of stuckness around a problem that they haven't brought to the surface of their own consciousness. They might know the solution is somewhere there, deep down inside, but they're not going deep enough to find it, like the dudes who decided not to bother trying to move the boulder out of their way.

Here are some examples to give you an overview of the process before we go into it in more detail in the next three chapters.

## Corporate Example

♦ **See It: Recognize the need for change.** A company notices that many customers are using Apple Pay to make purchases and that their competitors are offering Apple Pay as a payment option. The company is aware that Apple Pay offers a quick, secure, and convenient payment method that could enhance the customer experience.

♦ **Face It: Accept the reality of the situation.** This company has to acknowledge the potential challenges of integrating Apple Pay (or not) into their existing payment systems, looking at technical requirements, hardware upgrades, and interoperability issues with certain payment hardware. The company also needs to consider the resources needed for the change, such as setting up an account with a payment processor/gateway, and ensuring adequate cryptographic standards.

♦ **Fix It: Take action to implement the change.** Now the company will develop a detailed plan to integrate Apple Pay into their payment systems, communicating the change effectively to all stakeholders, and managing the transition process.

## Literary Example

♦ **See It:** Recognize the need for change. In the story of the Barefoot King, the king is walking on a rough path and his feet are sore.

♦ **Face It: Accept the reality of the situation.** He decides that he should cover the land with something soft so that nobody's feet will hurt as they walk throughout the kingdom.

◆ **Fix It: Take action to implement the change.** The minister's suggestion to change the king's shoes instead of the path represents a shift in perspective. It's about adapting oneself or internal processes to better deal with the external environment. In change management, this translates to developing new strategies, skills, or tools to handle challenges more effectively instead of expecting the external environment to accommodate one's current way of doing things.

This parable emphasizes the importance of recognizing when a change is needed (See It), understanding that the solution may come from altering one's own approach rather than the external circumstances (Face It), and then implementing the necessary changes to address the issue (Fix It). It teaches that sometimes the most effective way to manage change and get unstuck is not to insist on changing the world around us, but to adapt ourselves and our methods to better navigate the reality we face.

## Personal Example

◆ **See It.** If you want to effectively deal with the things that aren't working in your life, you have to bring them to the surface by being honest about the things that aren't working for you.

◆ **Face It.** Next, you have to face the fact that it is your responsibility to do something about the situation. You accept where you are, and you do not hate yourself because of it. You're facing the fact that you have to do something about it.

◆ **Fix It.** Here's where you take action. There is a time for theory and a time for practice. In the Fix It stage, there is no more thinking, no more data collection. There is nothing else. People consume themselves with what they need to do instead of doing it. That ends here.

My take on responsibility is to break it into two words: *response* and *ability*. You have the *ability* to *respond* in the future in whatever way you choose.

So what if you haven't dealt with your problems until now? Don't feel guilty about that. Don't blame anyone else or any set of circumstances. Take responsibility today, and decide how you want to move forward.

Awareness + Responsibility = Action

**This can generally only happen when you feel a certain amount of urgency.**

After you decide that you're able to respond to your problems, how do you light a fire under your ass to take action? You throw away the lid of the paint can. Let me explain.

You've decided it's time to paint your living room walls. Nobody really *wants* to spend a day painting their walls, but it has to be done from time to time. Once you get into the project, you might be tempted to paint one wall, put the lid back on the can, and take a break. While you're watching TV or scrolling social media, you may decide that one freshly painted wall is good enough. Or maybe you tell yourself you want some time to decide whether you like the new color. Meanwhile, the paint brushes are getting dry and crusty, the paint is starting to separate, and it will take a lot of work to get back into the groove. This is a great way to lose motivation. And even though you know the walls need to be painted, your brain will tell you they were fine the way they were.

My advice? Throw away the paint can lid, and paint the damn walls. Effort is the one thing we can control in life. If you always gave all the effort you had to give, your life would be way better. Don't let the paint dry until the walls have the final coat.

You might want to lose 20 pounds, but you also might not like the idea of working out every day and eating healthy. Nobody wants to do the process; everyone wants the benefit.

Of course, you don't want to paint your living room. I don't want you to paint the walls, either. I want you to enjoy the benefit of the walls being painted. Doing the work is not sexy.

I was recently at a dinner where someone posed the question, "What's your dream job?"

One guy laughed and said, "I don't dream of work."

Makes total sense. We don't dream of work; we dream of the results that working provides us.

If your walls don't need to be painted, then don't paint them.

In Chapter 1, you were honest with yourself about the real problem you were trying to solve.

Because you're reading this book, we know that something needs to be painted. Back when I was still hiding my hand, I knew that I needed to paint my wall. I'd been living with the color I hated for 17 years. But I didn't want to paint, so I put a bunch of furniture up and hung some posters so I couldn't see the issue.

That was easier than looking at the real issue. But it was only keeping me in pain for longer than I needed to be.

If you know you need to change something in your life but you can't find a wall to paint, you've either turned away from the wall or you're outside, running away from your problems.

Having ownership, accepting full responsibility, and taking action are going to get you unstuck. And that's why the "See It, Face It, Fix It" process is so damn good. That's what I'm going to talk about next.

**Dorothy:** If you were really great and powerful, you'd keep your promises!

**Oz's voice:** Do you presume to criticize the ....

MLS — Toto pulls back the curtain to reveal the Wizard at the controls of the throne apparatus.

# CHAPTER 6

# Step 1: Subconscious to Conscious

**KEY TASKS FROM THIS CHAPTER:**

- Identify the real issue.
- Use radical honesty to identify the real problems.
- Use the Five Whys to find the root problem.
- Write the problems down in detail.

Princess Ariel was fascinated by the human world. Despite warnings from her father, King Triton, Ariel dreamed of exploring the land above the sea. On one of her adventures, she witnessed a shipwreck during a storm and rescued a human, Prince Eric. The young mermaid princess fell in love with him and made a deal with the sea witch Ursula to become human so they could be together.

In exchange for legs, Ariel gave the sea witch her voice. This made it difficult for her to communicate with Eric, which was a problem because she was on a tight timeline. If she couldn't make Eric fall in love with her, Ursula would get to keep her soul.

Ariel had trouble adapting to her legs and the loss of her identity. But she was determined to make Eric fall in love with her and pursue her dream of living on land. Because of Ariel's determination and charm, Eric fell in love with her, just in time for Ursula to intervene, causing more problems for Ariel. With the help of her friends, Ariel was able to break the curse and reclaim her voice. But she was back in her mermaid form.

King Triton could see how much happier Ariel was with Eric and her legs, so he let her choose her own path and gave her his blessing to stay on land and marry her prince. Ariel ended up with the best of both worlds. She won Eric's love and the acceptance of her mermaid family.

*The Little Mermaid* is a good example of the "man in a hole" (or mermaid in a hole, in this case) story structure. The protagonist faces challenges and learns from their experience, ultimately finding a new, more fulfilling life. In other words, the character is going about their business, gets in trouble, and gets out again, returning to a new normal.

There's a good chance that you're currently in a hole. The process I'm about to take you through is going to help you climb out.

The success of the man in a hole plot is dependent on the main character learning something as a result of their time in the hole. There are tons of examples of the man in a hole story arc in film and literature: *Alice in Wonderland, The Wonderful Wizard of Oz, Cinderella, Finding Nemo*, and *Apollo 13*, to name a few. And there are plenty of examples in business, too.

Starbucks' Howard Schultz learned from backpacking across Europe that coffee shops in America could be more than just diners and donut shops.

Kutol was a soap manufacturing company that made a special wallpaper cleaner in the 1930s. When vinyl wallpapers hit the market, wallpaper cleaners became obsolete. Joe McVicker was a relative of one of Kutol's owners and thought their product made a good children's toy. Play-Doh was born.

Nintendo was founded in 1889 and started as a playing card company. The market for playing cards started to take a dip in the mid-20th century, posing a problem for Nintendo. They struggled to find a way to remain relevant until the original founder's grandson—Hiroshi Yamauchi—took over as president in 1949. He saw an opportunity to enter the video game industry. Donkey Kong hit arcades in the early 1980s. The rest is history.

Between the ages of 10 and 27, I was in a hole. I hid my hand in a glove because I thought that if I didn't acknowledge my disability, other people couldn't comment on it, either.

It was exhausting, but I hadn't allowed myself to imagine that there could be another way. I wasn't ready to climb out of the hole.

It's human nature to bury our problems to avoid pain. We spend an extraordinary amount of our energy pushing things down, as if pretending that we aren't suffering were enough to keep us out of pain.

But how can you face it and fix it if you can't see it?

**The first step of the Changing Course process is to acknowledge and feel the things you've been hiding from.**

A series of events led you to your current reality. It didn't just big bang theory its way into existence. Acceptance is understanding that this is just the way it has happened so far and that you have a role and responsibility in both getting here and getting out. It is ineffective to think of responsibility as blame or fault, but it is a hell of a lot easier to feel that way, feeling "accused" of causing your reality. I very much know other people, other environments, and other factors played a varying role in the shaping of your current reality. But I don't care about them right now—I care about helping you. You can't control what happened from outside forces. You can't even control what you did in the past. But what you can control is assessing the process that led to the path you're on right now and tweak your strategy. Taking responsibility is not about blame—it's about regaining power over your life when it feels as if you've spiraled out of control. Reclaiming your role and responsibility in uprighting your ship takes you from "I can't do this" to "It's my responsibility, so *how* can I do this?" Don't you think it's time to regain control of your life direction?

If so, this is what it takes: No more dishonesty. No more avoidance. No more ignoring the parts of you that you know you need to improve. You are not broken. You are not a bad leader or a bad person. You are a person who has survived by counterintuitively using the wrong tools for the job. No more playing basketball with a tennis racket—give yourself a chance to put down the strategies you know in exchange for the strategies to grow.

Everything changes when you start telling the truth and accepting where you are. And I mean radical honesty and radical acceptance. Telling 100% truth on 50% of the problem is still a lie. Using ineffective language to avoid acceptance will anchor you to your inefficiencies.

If you're unsatisfied with your mentality or habits, and you know that getting rid of the doubt, bitterness, negativity, procrastination, avoidance, numbness, and fear, among other ways you have of coping with life, are ineffective, then taking ownership of your real problems starts your course correction.

The following includes a set of rules for accomplishing radical honesty and radical accountability in all areas of your life. Use these rules in your exploration for your truth to help resist the urge to negotiate on the facts of any situation. Really understand these rules and give yourself permission to take them in regardless of any knee-jerk emotional reactions or resistance that may arise as you read them.

## Nine Rules for Radical Honesty and Acceptance

1. Rejecting reality does not change it.
2. Changing reality requires accepting it.
3. Discomfort can't be avoided.
4. Rejecting reality turns pain into suffering.
5. Refusing to accept reality will keep you stuck.
6. Ignoring bad habits worsens your reality.
7. Resisting ownership delays your progress.
8. Give up what you think you know for what you need to know.
9. You should not be anywhere other than where you currently are.

Honesty is either all-encompassing or nonexistent.

"A half-truth is the most cowardly of lies."

—*Mark Twain*

Avoidance, omission, hidden truth, white lies ... they're all forms of deceit. Deceit is not based on malice. You aren't lying to be a terrible person or particularly sinister. You could be smudging the whole truth because acknowledging that you might have made your experience worse with your own actions or inactions is a very painful thought. Discomfort and pain are unavoidable when uprooting what's familiar and practiced, regardless of the result being less than ideal. Our unwavering commitment to the devil we know dissuades us from accepting painful truths. However, that rejection of reality does not change reality but rather turns pain into suffering. In the context of taking into account what your real problems are, pain may be part of growth, but turning pain into suffering is avoidance leading to misery. You shouldn't be farther along or better at something or any other discouraging language aimed at rejecting the reality of your being exactly where you should be.

Mental inertia makes altering repeating patterns difficult. So if someone tells you that you need to accept your reality in order to begin changing the narratives and outcomes of your life, you may hear those words but not truly accept them. Instead, put pen to paper and see what you come up with. This problem-solving matrix is a pros-and-cons list of two conflicting ideas, methods, or behaviors. Based on your answers, this exercise can help you identify a combination of what to do and what not to do.

|      | Accepting where you are | Not accepting where you are |
|------|-------------------------|-----------------------------|
| Pros |                         |                             |
| Cons |                         |                             |

As a note, similar to the advice of not going grocery shopping when you're hungry, the exercises in this book produce their best results when you can sit with a calm, clear, and open mind. Being emotionally charged fresh out of an argument, negative spiral, or extreme event can make it difficult to want to see the effective versions of responses. It very well may be what you need in the moment to ground you, but I feel the need to note the potential influence a reactionary emotion can have.

So how do you go about being honest and operating with radical acceptance to turn an invisible force of resistance into a visible and viable problem that can be matched with a solution?

## The Discovery Process

The art of questioning with curiosity instead of judgment will help you identify the real problems that need to be addressed. This discovery process requires an equal balance of self-compassion and responsibility to effect change. Proper coexistence of removing judgment and treating yourself like someone you love with taking ownership of areas of improvement and actions required is crucial for growth and change management.

While there is not one be-all and end-all line of questioning that easily unlocks the answers you need, there are different methods to get to the root that serve to get you there. Whether you use some of the discovery question frameworks or just sit with yourself and truly write down the language, beliefs, habits, and choices that need to be corrected, bringing the subconscious problems to the surface and becoming uncomfortably conscious of them puts you in a position to act effectively. Step 1 starts now.

## Unmasking the Problem

Not everything is as it seems at the surface—but what sits at the surface gives you a place to start. The goal here is to use an existing issue to find *the* preexisting issue.

Some issues will be external. You might possess some ability to influence, but the real influence will come from what you can do to change your reactions and the way you perceive the external issue if all else fails. There's no way around a market collapse, an upper management shift, a partner committing to leaving, or a pandemic happening. We know that any of these disruptive changes are a problem. But we are not after finding a problem (I'm sure we could find millions if we tried); we are after finding *the* problem.

Radical acceptance positions you to accept what you can't control and what is. So what about this disruption is the real problem for you? How does this disruption affect your life? Are you using facts to describe the issue or strongly formed, emotionally charged opinions? What negative emotions and behaviors are you engaging in related to this disruption? What needs to be done? What's stopping you internally from doing what is effective or best for you?

Loss and disruption can lead to forms of pain at varying levels. You are human and allowed to feel, and moreover, you should feel these natural feelings. It is important to sit with what you feel emotionally. It is equally important to accept the factual reality. Doing both will help you validate the human side of hardships without getting lost in the deception of self-sabotage. There is no need to repeatedly and negatively narrate the past. The ownership aspect requires you to isolate what your real concerns and resistances are to changing with the change. These are the real problems—the problems you can solve and change.

Unmasking internal issues presents its own set of challenges. There is no urgency of external disruption, no push or catalyst for you to change. These issues can fester and strengthen how stuck you feel when left unmanaged.

To fix the issue, you have to find the issue that will require radical honesty with yourself:

- What kind of repeated distress or dissatisfaction are you experiencing in your life?
- What struggles do you find yourself hiding from people?
- What negative themes or behaviors (self-sabotage, avoidance, feeling helpless or like a victim, isolation, etc.) do you find recurring in your life?
- What is the main issue you've struggled with in your personal or professional life?

This phase, specifically isolating the internal issue, is particularly tricky because, as you get closer and closer to finding the root problem, your brain can sense that vulnerability as a threat and set off every alarm and security measure to keep you safe—except safe in this sense means stuck. As you inch toward seeing that you are not committing to the work because you're afraid to fail or too attached to comfort, which manifests as laziness or validation for subpar ownership of your life, the ego kicks and gets defensive.

The defensive ego is a dangerous one, using every tool to resist the raw truth:

"No, it's because of what happened last month/year."

"If that hadn't happened, then I wouldn't be where I am."

"Maybe I'm just not supposed to be happy."

"It is what it is, can't do anything about it."

"I'm just not good at it."

"I already know what I need to work on."

"It's really not that bad right now."

"This is just who I am; I've always done it this way."

"It worked for me in the past."

"I know what works best for me."

"I'm just too busy, tired, stressed, etc., to do something right now."

All of these are signs of resistance to change, serving to only cement you to an outcome you know you find unpleasant that you wish would somehow change. All forms of avoidance, excuses, and ineffective language need to be fact-checked and filtered to remove opinions and validations to stay stuck.

Blame does nothing for you. Pity does nothing for you. Avoidance does nothing for you. Dishonesty does nothing for you. Procrastination does nothing for you. You must be willing to see through the fog of defense mechanisms without emotionally investing in these distractions from the core problems.

Luckily, each negative or ineffective avoidance tactic can be processed by the Five Whys technique to further get to the real problem.

## Stop and Think

- ◆ What have you struggled to accept that might be hurting your growth?
- ◆ What might you be avoiding and why? How can that avoidance be hurting you?
- ◆ What themes do you see in your life that keep happening?
- ◆ What role might you play in those themes?
- ◆ How might your life improve if you were 100% honest with yourself about what you can do in your situation?

## The Five Whys Technique

When you find the real problem, but you are not exactly sure how to troubleshoot it, the Five Whys technique, developed by Toyota founder Sakichi Toyoda almost a century ago, is a great place to start. The simplicity of asking *why* five times (or as many as needed, honestly) can quickly help identify a singular root problem. Each *why* aims to dive a layer deeper to discover the underlying cause (Figure 6.1).

Here is a general scenario to see it in action:

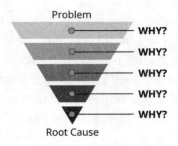

Figure 6.1 The Five Whys root cause analysis diagram.

**Problem:** I hate my life, but I'm not changing.

◆ Why #1: Why do you hate your life?

Because I feel unfulfilled in my job and personal life.

◆ Why #2: Why do you feel unfulfilled in your job and personal life?

Because I'm not pursuing my interests and I'm settling for a routine that doesn't excite me.

◆ Why #3: Why are you not pursuing your interests?

Because I don't think I have the time or resources.

◆ Why #4: Why don't you think you have time or resources?

Because I haven't sat down and seriously assessed my schedule or finances to find ways to make that change work.

◆ Why #5: Why haven't you assessed your schedule or finances?

Because the idea of changing is scary and the possibility of failing does not motivate me to take the first step.

In this specific instance, while the problem topically seemed to be that the person hated their life, the root of the problem was fear of change and failure, demotivating them to take the initial and necessary steps to even find ways to change, let alone commit to making those necessary changes.

Getting to the root here would turn an overwhelming feeling of "I hate my life" into "The issue is not that I'm unhappy in my life but rather that I'm resisting change because I'm afraid and unmotivated to try." The course of action here would be to face that fear and talk about it with someone you respect (more on this in the next chapter) and create an easy-to-execute plan of manageable steps toward change, which would not only help reduce the perceived risk of failure but also add accomplishments along the way to reinforce that effective behavior. That plan here could include setting aside one uninterrupted hour a week to plan out a schedule and financial snapshot to see where they have space and in what resource capacity. From there, maybe they decide that they have five hours a week to dedicate to a new job search and get back to some personal interests.

Here are a few prompts you can start with when using the Five Whys:

- What problem are you currently facing in your personal life?
- What problem are you currently facing in your professional life?
- Why are you feeling stuck?
- Are you content with your personal life? Professional life? Health? Wealth?
- What do you wish you could change most?

Any real assessment of where you are and what you are struggling with can prompt the Five Whys technique to get to the root of the issue. From mindset to confidence to leadership to sales to reinventing any aspect of your world, your ability to fix problems is directly proportional to your ability to find out why.

## Excruciate the Details

Check any résumé, and you'll find some rendition of the phrase "detail-oriented problem solver." In the world of creating and sustaining change, solving problems can be like working hard or studying all night long—acting ineffectively creates more work that often gets incorrectly rewarded. Working hard is only great if you're working effectively. Studying all night sounds like commitment unless it's a consequence of poor time management leading up to the test. Similarly, there's no use in solving problem after problem if solving the main problem would eliminate the need to solve the other problems. If every major muscle in your body feels tight, it's tempting to stretch each muscle until the tightness goes away, and when it comes back you repeat the process in this seemingly endless case of putting out small fires. It's not until you zoom out from solving the small problems and zoom in to finding the big problems that you realize you've been standing barefoot on ice, causing your entire body to tighten up. So now you realize tightness is not the problem; standing on bare ice is.

**Instead of just being a problem solver, you have to become a detail-oriented problem identifier.** That requires problem precision. In the following process, excruciate the details in each stage to truly identify the real problem. For example, instead of saying, "I'm lazy," dig deeper in detail: "I procrastinate and doom-scroll on my phone because it feels nice at first, but then I get lost in social media and lose track of time" or "It's much easier to stay in and watch Netflix than go to the gym, so I delay exercising with one more episode, and then say I have to cook and clean, and then it's too late, so I don't go." By having more detail, you can shift from ineffective topical problems to real issues and real barriers you can tackle.

---

Describe the problem behavior: _____.
Describe the prompting event: _____.
Describe the factors before the event making you vulnerable:
_____.
Describe the chain of events and resulting action and feeling:
_____.

---

Not only will the details of the problem provide you a place to implement small changes in the optimal direction, but identifying environments and triggers of the problem, as well as results, will help you catch the problem before it happens or as it happens and motivate you to change it because you've considered the results and clearly see how it's doing more harm than good.

## What Exists in the Shadows

Up until now, we've acknowledged that we can't fix what we aren't willing to face. What lies on the outskirts of that sentiment are the shadows that really suck to even glance at out of fear of actualization. The subconscious thoughts loom just outside of our current awareness, but the unconscious thoughts sit suppressed in the shadows of your mind.

I've come to understand the subconscious mind as all that exists just outside the focal point of your direct consciousness: the position of your feet right now, the texture on that painting, the faint sound you can find if you search for it. Your unconscious mind is where your shadow self exists according to psychoanalyst Carl Jung. That shadow acts as a reservoir for repressed feelings, experiences, desires, and beliefs, proving difficult to recognize immediately. Jung's work on shadow reveals that the way we present ourselves to the world acts as a mask. That mask is often the opposing and contrarian ideologies we suppress in our shadow side. This can come in the form of disliking someone for being so outgoing or happy when, deep down, you wish you were more outgoing and happy. It can also present as disliking certain traits other people have as a mask to avoid realizing you act the same way. It is natural to have inner conflict in our psyche, but Jung notes that the shadow self often manifests in projections to the world. These projections are defense mechanisms where feelings are directed toward someone or something else when, in reality, they are reflections of themselves. This could be an executive who blames their team for not listening or understanding yet struggles to effectively communicate and doesn't actively listen to others. This could also be a person who struggles with self-confidence but body-shames and judges other people.

Repression may serve to protect you from feeling overwhelmed by relived trauma and distress, but the unmanaged projections and shadow can negatively affect your behavior seemingly out of nowhere without a reason. Jung, writing on the shadow, noted that these issues "are bound to come to light in us, should we wish—as we ought—to live without self-deception or self-delusion" (Jung 1963). And while these deep-rooted unconscious struggles might not be able to be permanently deleted from your psyche, exploration and self-reflection on the root issue can reduce the chaos that can come from these darker parts of us, giving you a modicum of control over an issue you are now more aware exists.

Here are some shadow work questions that can help you self-reflect on core issues that might be hiding even below your subconscious mind:

- ◆ What are some of my pet peeves about other people? Do I see these pet peeves in my own behavior?
- ◆ What is something that I always complain about and why? What ownership do I have in the situation?
- ◆ What are my most toxic traits?
- ◆ What personal vices do I wish I had more control over?
- ◆ What needs do my vices satisfy?
- ◆ What do I need to learn about myself?
- ◆ What are my fears, and how do they affect me?
- ◆ What is something my younger self needed but never received?
- ◆ What are some of my past emotions relating to fear, security, safety, and anxiety?
- ◆ What are the patterns and beliefs that have been shaping my life?

- What recurring patterns or themes do I notice in my life that seem to hold me back or cause me distress?
- Can I think of a time when I felt most alive and engaged? What was different about that time compared to now?
- What are the fears or anxieties that I have that might be rooted in my unconscious mind?
- What aspects of myself do I find unacceptable or wish to change, and why do I think that is?
- Are there any emotions or feelings that I find myself avoiding or suppressing? If so, what are they?
- What do I judge harshly about others that might actually reflect something about myself that I do not want to acknowledge?
- What dreams or ambitions have I given up on, and what were the reasons for letting them go?
- In what ways do I find myself behaving in a self-sabotaging manner, and what might be the underlying reasons for this behavior?
- How do I typically react to criticism or failure, and what does this reveal about my deeper insecurities or beliefs?
- What is one day or moment I wish to forget, and how is that possibly still affecting me?

Some of these different question methodologies overlap intentionally. Think back to when you were a kid being asked to clean your room. You know damn well you didn't do it the first or fifth time you were asked until you were chased around the house with a lopsided broom by your patience-drained mom (just me?). I want you to repeat these questions. I want you to repeatedly answer them. Your job here is to become undeniably aware of what the real problems are. That discovery process is about using specific recollection of facts—not interpretations or opinions—to home in on what truly needs to be seen, faced, and, later in this process, fixed.

The realization of your resistance to change provides you an opportunity to detach yourself from the anchor that has no plans of ever being unstuck. You've got to put pen, pencil, or crayon to paper, though.

## Do It *Write* Now

Effective change management needs to be accessible, as does problem identification. In gathering the facts and asking the questions, having the uncomfortable conversations with yourself to pinpoint the real issues, you need to do something with your results. The simplest way to transition the intangible subconscious issues into tangible conscious issues is by writing them down.

In terms of accessibility, you don't need to buy an expensive journal or write in calligraphy on a psychoanalytic Sigmund Freud couch. You don't even necessarily need to write—you can type, use voice-to-text, scribble, or use any form of taking what's on the inside of your brain and making it real in the outside world.

Aside from the accessible step to turn thought into thing, writing ideas down only further helps you to remember, act, accomplish, and manage various aspects of navigating your new course. Studies out of Dominican University note that participants who put pen to paper and wrote down their goals were 42 percent more likely to accomplish those goals compared to their ruminating counterparts. And beyond goal setting, the neuroscience behind writing things down says that encoding (which is the process of sending perceived thoughts or ideas to the hippocampus, a region of the brain that helps determine what we learn, remember, and forget) is improved. By writing it down, you increase the likelihood of learning it and remembering it. Reflecting through writing, often referred to as journaling, has been an effective strategy for people to identify and regulate behaviors and emotions during their self-reflections as well, allowing people to revisit past thought patterns instead of assuming they remember everything they were thinking and feeling in the past.

You can have upward of 60,000 thoughts a day. A reported 80 percent of those thoughts can be considered negative, and an even higher percentage of those thoughts are repetitive. Getting lost in thought happens. With all that you have going on in your personal life, your career, your health, and your brain, it's exceedingly easier to "think so much that you sink." You try to partially address all the thoughts you have that keep you from truly making any progress. This is where writing down and encoding your priority problems helps you focus on turning random negative thoughts into intentional steps toward no longer staying stuck.

This phase involves writing. You have to be an active participant in your own improvement.

**The medium is not important. It's about bringing your problem up from the recesses of your brain and into the real world, taking it from subconscious to conscious.**

Don't expect to solve your problem at this point, though. This is just about bringing things to the surface where you can see them. Unfortunately, your problems won't just magically solve themselves by doing 33% of the work. You have to develop awareness and open your mind to the possibility of solving your problem instead of hiding or ignoring it.

To change, you have to be vulnerable. Surgery, car repair, and home renovation are everyday examples of situations requiring vulnerability to get to the root of the issue in order to create effective change.

You have to understand that change might be uncomfortable, but staying stuck will be worse. Just because you're comfortable staying stuck doesn't mean you should stay there.

A commitment to staying stuck is a fixed mindset. And while no one in their right mind commits to staying stuck, the lack of

pursuit in finding the truth becomes an inadvertent commitment to stagnation. Left unidentified, these deeper problems
will have you pointing fingers at the complications stemming
from the real issues rather than the real issues themselves. The
problem is not the low tire pressure light in the car. The problem is your tire flew off three miles back, and you tried to
keep going.

Step 1 is being conscious of your problem.

This is why I like writing them down in some way, whether
a mind map or a Venn diagram or a pros-and-cons list. It could
be journaling or a freeform Q&A, or you can use the work-
sheets I have available for free at https://artofchangingcourse
.com.

Be direct. Be honest. Be curious. Be nonjudgmental. This is
the situation: [PROBLEM] sucks. I don't like [PROBLEM], but
[PROBLEM] is the reality of what I've been running from.
[PROBLEM] is where I currently am. Here are the facts. Here are
some problems, and here are *the* problems. Here are the patterns and scenarios that keep recurring. Here is my role in
[PROBLEM]. When I fix [PROBLEM] one or more areas of my
life will greatly improve. I haven't fixed [PROBLEM] yet, but
I am willing to no longer be who I used to be. I am not this
[PROBLEM]. I am not the pattern of this [PROBLEM]. My potential will no longer be limited by [PROBLEM]. I am willing to
change course.

Most people can't take honest ownership of where they are.
They minimize it, lie about it, ignore it, or do anything but be
honest about where they are. Or what currently is. Give yourself enough grace to see the truth without disparaging yourself
but enough responsibility to recognize your role in what got
you here and what it will take to get you out.

**Warning: Don't get stuck at this step.**

So many people stop at the journaling and problem identification phase and fail to continue onward and take action.

Listen, if you've been journaling for five years about the same problem, it's time to move on to the next step. Don't get stuck in the hole, going from subconscious to conscious to subconscious again. I've been there, too, and it's one of the common pitfalls I address toward the end of this book. Awareness and knowledge without action get you nowhere, leading only to a progress-less path littered with the guilt and shame that comes from recognizing a problem and doing nothing about it.

If you don't complete this step honestly and thoroughly, the rest of this book is meaningless. You don't need more knowledge on what else you could do. You owe it to yourself and the impact you could be having on those around you to harness what you know and lean in to your willingness to act. Whether it takes you ten minutes, a week, or a month, you have to get to the root of the real problem.

To do this, you must see and name the feeling and problem you're struggling with. If your problem stops at a generality such as, "I want to be healthy" or "I want to work harder," that's good, but it's still not the deep feeling and issue you're looking for.

Go back to Chapter 1 and make sure you've identified your real problem. Then reread Chapter 2 to see how your brain is trying to keep you stuck. Then review Chapter 3, and see how you're talking about this problem so language isn't getting in the way.

You have to accept yourself. Your *true* self.

Instead of constantly saying you need to change, you need to better yourself, you need to improve; just stop. You need to focus on the root problems. Yes, when the tire goes flat, you need to change it, but saying you need to change it 60 times does nothing for you compared to getting out of the car, pulling out the spare, and getting to work.

Imagine having a friend or boss who constantly ridicules you for who you are. "You need to be different." "You need to change." "You need to improve everything." "Nothing you do is good, and you need to do better."

How comfortable would you feel in their presence? Would you be eager to produce or even say anything? Not only would I be pissed (and probably avoid changing out of spite), but I'd be conditioned to believe them and I'd be afraid of doing anything out of fear that I'd mess it up because I wasn't good enough.

That's the environment you create in your head when you continually bash yourself for your shortcomings, an environment lacking in self-trust and self-belief and devoid of confidence or opportunity to change.

The desire to change does not have to be black and white or extreme. It's not a "beat yourself up or coddle yourself into complacency" situation. Own your role without attacking your character. Write the radically honest truth about what has been going on, and be willing to face it.

When you're satisfied that you've brought your problem from subconscious to conscious, it's time for Step 2 of the process: conscious → communicated.

| | |
|---|---|
| **Dorothy:** | Oh, will you help me? Can you help me? |
| **Glinda:** | You don't need to be helped any longer. You've always had the power to go back to Kansas. |
| **Dorothy:** | I have? |
| **Scarecrow:** | Then why didn't you tell her before? |
| **Glinda:** | Because she wouldn't have believed me. She had to learn it for herself. |
| **Tin Man:** | What have you learned, Dorothy? |
| **Dorothy:** | I won't look any further than my own backyard. Because if it isn't there, I never really lost it to begin with! Is that right? |
| **Glinda:** | That's all it is! |

# CHAPTER 7

# Step 2: Conscious to Communicated

**KEY TASKS FROM THIS CHAPTER:**

- Balance self-reliance and getting help.
- See asking for help as a strength and benefit to others, too.
- Be willing to make and keep reasonable commitments.
- Compare commitment to change to commitment to staying stuck.
- Communicate your problems and commitments to someone else.
- Hold yourself accountable personally and with help from others.

A man stops to visit his friend, and they have a chat on the porch. To their right, a dog is softly whimpering.

"What's wrong with your dog?" asks the visiting friend.

"Oh, he's lying on a rusty nail. Every time I go to fix it, he just lays on it again."

"Why doesn't he get up?"

"I guess it doesn't hurt enough."

Have you ever felt as if you had to be everything to everyone? As if you had to be strong or indestructible for the people around you whether at work or in your everyday life? You might feel this obligation to portray strength and success even if something deep down is heavily weighing on you. And sometimes you may question how long you'll be able to keep this up before you break.

Like the dog in this scenario, it's alarmingly easy to become so connected to your processes and habits that you normalize even the most dysfunctional patterns that hurt you. Your ability to adapt even to pain makes the nail in your life go from painful to bearable to normal to "comfortably uncomfortable."

Being stuck is a constant state of living comfortably uncomfortable. Even when you're offered help to potentially exit that undesired state, you refuse or avoid the offer. Like a thermostat set to 75 degrees, you can open the door, which attempts to lower the temperature, or have a party, which attempts to raise the temperature, but regardless, the thermostat will work overtime to make sure it stays exactly where it is set. The harder you try to alter the temperature, the harder the thermostat fights you to return to its programmed state. Passive decisions and indecisions to retain familiarity act as the thermostat in this case. You make every attempt to change temporarily—only to return to your default state shortly after.

The thermostat has to change. And knowing the root problem isn't enough. Sometimes you just genuinely need help.

In Chapter 6, you took your problem from subconscious to conscious. Limited self-awareness and ownership can delay you in seeking help and acting, so now you've minimized that first barrier to change. It's a great start, and it means you have a solid platform for change. But having a platform for change doesn't guarantee a transformation.

Here's where accountability comes in to encourage action and adherence, by communicating the issue to someone you trust and value. Accountability is the act of being responsible or held to account for your actions and commitments—whether by yourself or also an accountability partner. Identifying the real problem and being willing to hold yourself accountable will drastically increase the success of short-term and long-term change. Through motivation to commit and tracking progress you gave your word on, you position yourself to disrupt the forces that kept you stuck so you can finally alter your course to a more desirable way of life.

Unfortunately, another barrier to change arises when considering getting help.

## Captain Crewless

Society today, especially Western culture, is dominated by the "one man/woman army" mentality alongside the "I don't need anybody but myself" mindset. The focus of self-reliance can be inspiring and empowering, influencing some pretty resilient behaviors and adaptation to challenging times. The problem becomes the erosion of asking for help when you actually need it, believing in the false absolutism of "me against the world." Even the less aggressive mentality and promotion of "self-care" reinforces the idea that all care of self is to be done by yourself, still implying the philosophy that it is solely on you to sort out your struggles. But perhaps there is more to self-care than merely caring for only yourself.

Since the literal dawn of time, the human species and every other surviving species have heavily relied on interdependence or just being connected with others to help when needed. From cave people to Neanderthals to different hunter gatherer societies to Okinawans who are among the longest living populations currently, connectedness and interdependence in combination of self-determination helped these societies survive and socially collaborate. The ancient populations are often misrepresented by merely brute force and extremely limited gender and ability roles, yet archeological evidence actually shows a much more egalitarian nature than we once thought, as some big game hunters were actually women, and people with disability in these different groups were often provided and cared for. Evidence shows that their value on vulnerability to an extent, as well as cooperation rather than self-reliance, allowed them to thrive given the limited resources they had.

The cornerstone of social structure has always been interdependence and value in helping others, and it only makes sense—just as you wouldn't close your eyes when mountain biking (I mean, I hope you wouldn't), why would you willingly give up resources that contribute to your success on a path that will undoubtedly vary in difficulty as you live your life? The division of interdependence and self-reliance is definitely a product of modern culture shifts. And with that culture shift comes the issues we need to tackle if we truly want change to happen, let alone stick.

Self-determination and self-reliance are vital for personal progress. Great leaders, partners, wives, employees, and people who succeed in any area of their lives all utilize an internal action-based approach. Prioritization of self-reliance alone, though, has painted a negative picture on asking for and getting help. Somewhere along the line, asking for help became a perceived sign of weakness.

The tough "do it all by myself" attitude has created this list of exhausting obligations: Only present yourself as an image of strength. Suppress negative emotion. Don't ever depend on others. Prioritize giving care, not getting it. It is almost as if I cannot accomplish it myself and I feel obligated to suffer due to my inadequacy and "suck it up." The stigma of getting help influences millions of people to feel they have to solve it themselves or suffer in silence. If you can't solve it, just cope like a normal Western adult, right? Alcohol and substances, food, isolation, lashing out and projecting—basically deal with it, but don't you dare ask for help. But where does this maladaptive behavior come from if connectedness is part of our instinctual process?

## Cultural Influences

I generally hate absolutes such as the phrase "geography is destiny" because there are varying degrees of truth to them, but there is a lot more truth in the phrase "geography is influence." Influences can come from where you were born but also your culture, nationality, parental beliefs, and overall environment. You have been influenced by a wide variety of surrounding ideas. Certain cultures promote more interdependence while others may promote less.

In many Latin cultures, family connectedness is embraced and valued, but the culture might be less supportive of going outside the family for help or advice. Certain cultures might have polarizing views on topics such as mental health, family values, work–life balance, and more, potentially preventing someone from seeking help.

In African American culture, certain stigmas around seeking help, especially around health and mental health, might exist due to lack of trust or accessibility in quality services, as well as a lack of ethnically sensitive and experienced providers. Past generational experiences can influence how you might choose to seek help.

Barriers of assistance can be passed down into all cultures and taught directly or indirectly through the way everyone around you acts during hardships. Assistance is a normal part of the human experience and not reserved for any one culture.

## Social Influences

The strange dichotomy that exists between social mutual support and self-reliance creates a very conflicting challenge. Overemphasis on self-reliance can cause relationship deterioration and isolation, effectively limiting mutual support. Perceived weakness from asking for help can affect your ability to acknowledge problems yourself, let alone discuss them, out of fear of being viewed as weak, incompetent, or inferior to your peers. Even children as young as seven have been found to share this belief. A degree of embarrassment or shame can coincide with expressing your need for help as well. In today's social currency, any negative remark on someone's character is seen as a red flag. Asking for help can be perceived socially as a negative. Ironically, not getting the help you need is the *actual* red flag.

Whether it feels like weakness or embarrassment, or it's just generally not encouraged, the social barriers that exist today can demotivate you to ever ask for the help you need.

## Educational Influences

Every system has its flaws. Addressing them does not negate their benefits. The modern education system can really reinforce the overly self-reliant student. Self-sacrifice in school, whether project- or test-based, almost seems to reward ruining your mental health to earn the validation of your teachers and the highly coveted A+ rating of your grades that low-key becomes the rating of your worth. While tutoring is broadly available, socio-educational stigmas and attitudes toward getting assistance are often mischaracterized, causing students to see tutoring only for people who have learning difficulties or are just incompetent. Basically, the negative stigma is the incorrect association that "intelligent people don't need help" and "only stupid people need tutoring." Along with perceived incompetence or self-stigma, fear of failing even after getting help acts as a big blockade to seeking help in education as well (Robert and Thomson 1994).

## Workplace Influences

Overworking and the "whatever it takes" attitude often create an accepted and embraced idea that struggling and burning yourself out is normal. Doing whatever it takes usually involves some work afterhours and working on weekends, which is not "forced" but can be rewarded. Normalizing overworking creates an accepted state of struggle. Fear of perceived incompetence and job security plays a role in people at work avoiding the idea of seeking assistance. Fast-paced environments, as well as careers of any caliber, can have this looming feeling that if you need to ask for help, you will be seen as weak or not the right person for the job. Maybe that could socially distance you from the cool kids at the watercooler. Or worse, it could threaten your financial security and job. The risks and perceived stigmas of help-seeking in the workplace can dissuade an employee from getting the growth they need.

Along with these individual areas, there is also the intersectionality of influences, creating a ripple effect throughout all aspects of your life. In an early study on minorities in education, researchers reported students of color who needed help felt getting help would be "discrediting" to them, so they refused. This can also be the case where you learned early in school that help is not what "good" students need, so now that overemphasis on self-reliance carries over into your personal and professional life, influencing you to lean more toward burnout, avoidance, and sacrificing your mental health instead of asking for help.

Shelly notices some of the other students in her third grade science class are able to answer questions she cannot and she needs help. While she doesn't realize that their parents have jobs in that science field and they regularly study one hour a day with them, she just incorrectly assumes they are smart and she is dumb. She doesn't want to be seen as dumb, so she doesn't ask questions or get help. This becomes a habit throughout school, limiting her from learning what doesn't come "naturally" to her. Shelly starts to develop coping mechanisms to make up for the help she needs by avoiding areas of unfamiliarity and sticking to what she knows, limiting her effort to expand her knowledge. This comfort of her knowledge quickly becomes a cage, limiting her ability to get higher-paying jobs and climb the ranks in any job she does find that matches her immovable skill set. She is set in her ways and very difficult to work with as outside perspective and advice are met with cognitive dissonance and dismissal. She begins to cling to rhetoric that validates her resistance to ask for help. "This is just who I am," she says. "This is how I've always done it, so either take it or leave it." Shelly knows her life isn't turning out to be what she hoped for. But until she decides to acknowledge what she needs and accept the truth that change might be needed, it will be easy for Shelly to stay stuck where she is in life.

The cultural and social influences can permeate every area of your life due to a combination of factors: lived experience, stigma, fear, avoidance, shame, vulnerability, and perception.

As we previously discussed, unmanaged narratives that haven't been filtered for the truth can be damaging. This again shows to be true as the majority of these concerns tend to be exaggerated or just flat out incorrect.

## Getting Is Also Giving

Leave it to our funky, maladaptive brains to use every illogical reason in the world for why asking for help is bad. On the one hand, we all love those motivational videos on social media showing people being genuinely helped. I immediately think of Zachery Dereniowski, better known as @mdmotivator on Instagram, who turned his life around from depression and isolation to now helping people down on their luck in such a beautiful way. With over $2 million given to complete strangers and over 17 million followers on social media, Zachery generally approaches people asking for a little help himself, and even people struggling the most offer to help. In turn, he returns that honest aid and often gives them some sort of life-changing gift. Watching the expressions of gratitude on these people's faces is emotional, but on top of that, the comments show people are inspired to follow his lead as well. As humans, it's hard not to smile at seeing someone genuinely get help, especially if you are the one helping. Unfortunately, when we become the ones needing help, we somehow forget how nice it is to help someone else.

When we start considering what motivates other people, we skew the narrative negatively, applying a much more pessimistic, self-centered view of the world. Forgetting your own enjoyment of helping others, you convince yourself it is somehow wrong and inconvenient to get help as it must be a burden no one else would be willing to bear. The need for assistance can instinctually have you retreat to your former negatively charged ineffective language model unless you hold strong to the facts. Assisting others not only can increase the overall happiness of the giver and elevate their own feelings of competence in their ability to help; it just seems to be a common intuitive response to help others and support people where they reasonably can. People who are invited to help and able to help in any way derive a personal sense of satisfaction from being asked to help. Neurochemically, the help they give can be communicated to their brain as a reward, activating the same parts of the brain that activities such as food and sex do. You are actively contributing to their overall contentment, validation, and general feel-good activity by seeking their assistance. They can feel a sense of purpose and fulfillment as well as a mood boost. Not to mention, by helping you, they can potentially lower their risk of depression and improve their overall life satisfaction.

Let's say a friend comes to you and tells you they don't trust many people to talk about their problems, but they trust you. How does that make you feel? They tell you this deep-rooted problem they've struggled with nearly their entire life. As you listen, you can tell they're opening up, and they feel very comfortable and safe speaking to you. How does that make you feel? They ask for your advice, and you provide a perspective they've never considered. You see their face light up with hope, near the point of tears. For the first time in their life, they feel seen and heard. And more important, they feel a sense of hope. They leave excited, with their head held high, and you can tell you helped them reach a turning point in their life with a simple conversation. How does that make you feel knowing you were trusted and you helped them with something extremely meaningful to them?

Pretty damn good, I bet.

Those great feelings you felt are what you can give to someone else by allowing them to help you. Consider Table 7.1 when asking for help, and allow yourself to consider alternative perspectives from your concerns.

**Table 7.1**   When Asking for Help

| Concern | Reality |
| --- | --- |
| "I'm afraid of looking incompetent." | "You're such a problem solver!" |
| "I'd hate to seem weak." | "You're brave." |
| "I'm scared of seeming dependent." | "You're quite the team player." |
| "What if I look dumb?" | "Thank you for taking accountability for your knowledge gap." |
| "It's not normal to struggle." | "There is no growth without struggle." |
| "I don't want to feel embarrassed." | "It takes strength to take ownership of your needs." |
| "This is going to be painful." | "You can't grow without *some* discomfort." |
| "I hate burdening people." | "Thank you for allowing me to help you." |
| "What if it's inconvenient?" | "Unresolved problems are more inconvenient." |
| "I'll probably fail anyway." | "Getting started reduces the likelihood of failing." |
| "I could lose status." | "I respect your vulnerability." |

You have to stop underestimating people's willingness to help and stop overestimating the things you "need" to do all by yourself.

Somewhere along the line, though, we've resisted the reality that paradoxical truths exist: You can be kind to yourself but still own up to your mistakes. Just as an ocean and a single wave are one and the same, self-reliance and interdependence can exist without canceling each other out. In fact, real change will come when you fully accept both truths and understand that both personal commitment and accountability are the vessels required to get out of port.

## Commitment

What do you feel when you hear the word "commitment"? You might shudder at the thought, associating it with being locked down by a task or job by force. Or you might drop your head in guilt, recalling all the times you said you were going to do something but never followed through. Commitment is a promise to yourself that you're willing and able to do what you say you will do. You bind yourself to a course of action that bridges the gap between promise and reality.

Regardless of your relationship to commitment in the past, your ability to create and pledge yourself to your commitments now will correlate with your ending up with the outcomes you want.

The first logical step would seem to be creating new commitments, right? Those new commitments are coming, but before that, you need to make some room for them by decluttering some of the prior commitments you already have.

Recall from Chapter 4 the importance of identifying competing commitments that might get in the way of your new commitments. The way forward requires you to fully—not partially—commit yourself to effective actions. When change begins, whether internal or external, there is a natural tendency to fall back to prior commitments. In the past, you may have committed to believing your feelings are facts or that you already know outcomes of actions you've never consistently taken. Or maybe those prior commitments are not as deeply philosophical and are just more automated. You committed to eating whatever you want, doing whatever you want, or speaking to yourself however you want regardless of consequence. Adding new commitments without dismantling old ones can just create frustration and conflict for you, adding resistance and risk to the new behaviors you really want.

The power of subtraction can really help create a neutral starting point instead of operating from a negative position. Clearing commitments that can hijack your progress can be your first real commitment so that your changes have the best opportunity to stick.

Whether you are preparing surfaces for adhesives or paint, a strong bond requires that the surface be prepped and cleaned of any former debris and grease that might still be there, even the dirt that might not be immediately visible. Sometimes you will need to aggressively sand the surface, getting rid of what used to be there to make sure the new bond will stick. Preparing the area by removing all the former gunk is the most important aspect of ensuring a strong, reliable bond. To prepare for your bond or commitment to change, you similarly have to rid yourself of debris from prior commitments so that these new commitments adhere as sturdily and reliably as possible.

You may want to start learning a new skill that can help you explore a new career path, so you decide you are going to spend two hours a day learning after work. That new commitment is met with resistance from your old commitment of playing video games as soon as you come home, creating a competition between knowing what you ultimately want and instant gratification of what you just want right now. The new commitment doesn't require you to abandon video games, though, just the idea that you get to play as soon as you get home and for however long you want. The best scenario is removing that old commitment and replacing it with the new one so that after you accomplish your new commitment, you are free to play.

Use the following chart to decide what will work best for you. Make sure you list both the logical outcomes and the feelings associated with those outcomes to assess the best choice and motivate the most effective move for you.

|      | Committing to new change | Committing to old ways |
|------|--------------------------|------------------------|
| Pros |                          |                        |
| Cons |                          |                        |

Have you ever stopped to think about what you are currently committed to doing? Yes, we all are aware of commitment being this big thing such as being committed to your partner or taking a "commitment to excellence" at work (whatever that means). But it's not usually the big commitments that have the greatest effect on us. The small, consistent commitments you make daily play a much greater role in your habits and behaviors than the one-off commitments you might make haphazardly.

My dad loved his commitments. He had a 45-minute drive to work as a registered nurse when I was growing up. He's a very particular man, and he enjoys the processes he has come to know. I'll never forget going to work with him one day, on one of those "bring your kid to work" days. The alarm went off at three in the morning, not because he needed to leave soon but rather to give him "an extra two hours of sleep" before he needed to be up at five. We were about 30 minutes into our drive as he prophesied every aspect of the drive: "Four seconds after we pass under this bridge in this lane, we will feel two slight bumps in the road," he'd say, "and right over there, you'll see a police cruiser that's empty, tucked away." I was thoroughly impressed (and maybe a little concerned!), but I also thought about how much he was committed to keeping his process the same. Expectation, familiarity, and just how he has always done it fueled these little decisions in his life. He never really thought much of it, but it always made me question what else people commit to.

What if, instead of completely reinventing yourself all at once (an impossible and defeating task), you simply committed to spending the first hour of your day knocking out the tasks you need to do but normally avoid? What if, instead of committing to a daunting weight loss goal that would take months or even a year, you committed to working out wherever you can (gym, home, hotel, etc.) at least twice a week? What if, instead of needing to change your entire life, you chose one action you could commit to today and every day that would move the needle not essentially far but just forward?

One of the biggest barriers to commitment and action is thinking, "If I can't do it all, then some is not enough, so I just won't do anything." Just listen to how illogical that is: Because you can't fix everything, you discredit fixing anything, leaving you with nothing in terms of progress?

We're naturally impatient and impulsive at times. That can lead us to take the misguided all-or-nothing approach that seems to come across as awesome and hardcore but often just doesn't really pan out. Imagine wanting to invest money but only having $10 to do so. It would be ridiculously easy to convince yourself that $10 won't do anything for you and that amount is a waste of time. Yet, none of that is true when you look at the big picture. Let's say you had put that measly $10 in Bitcoin in 2010. That "useless" $10 would have gotten you roughly 12,000 Bitcoin, which would now be worth over $600 million. This is an extreme example, but if you had taken that $10 and invested it in the beginning of any major stock, undoubtedly, you'd see a large percentage of gain over time by simply putting in what you can afford into a seemingly positive investment.

But let's make it even more practical: If you set aside $10 a week, and then increase that savings as and when you can, and you invest in, say, an S&P 500 index fund, you'll see an average annual rate of return of around 10%. Twenty years of $10 a week in this scenario could yield upward of $30,000. Over time, your modest monthly investments will snowball.

I won't pretend to know financial investing, so here is an alternative scenario I know all too well. When people used to hire me to help them get in shape, they would be motivated to acknowledge these lofty goals that they undoubtedly wanted to achieve: "I want to lose 50 pounds! I'm committing to losing 50 pounds and going to the gym every single day for three hours, and I'm committing to only eating kale!" There are two major problems with the commitments here: separating outcome from commitment and overcommitting.

## Outcome Is Not Commitment

I've always had a distaste for setting only outcome-based goals, let alone commitments. The dopamine release you get from writing down that big outcome goal feels nice, but it also creates a faraway finish line that you will not cross for some time. That's why it's also important to create finish lines daily in the form of commitments to daily actions, not outcomes. While I know my clients' mission was to lose weight (for a deeper purpose we'd discover in the subconscious → conscious phase), I helped reframe my clients' commitment from focusing on the distance mission to focusing on the small tasks they needed to accomplish today. We changed the vague commitment to the long-term mission to a specific commitment of "I commit to logging what I eat and limiting my portions" and "I commit to getting my steps in every day." By creating those daily finish lines, they didn't have to wait until they lost 50 pounds to feel accomplished or proud—they felt that every day, which further reinforced their commitment to the overall mission.

Of course, you want to be stress-free. Of course you want a high-paying career change. Of course, you want unwavering confidence, the perfect partner, or the physique of a Greek god. There is nothing wrong with the outcome you want, especially after identifying what the real problem is. But a vague commitment without digestible and realistic-for-you action steps will be more temporary than transformational. Your decision to commit to the small actions that move you in the right direction will gradually lead you to the larger goal or outcome.

Here are a few questions to help you establish your commitments:

◆ What is the real problem?
◆ What is the ultimate outcome?
◆ What is the simplest first step that you can 100% do?
◆ Are you willing to commit to that first step?
◆ What might stop you from doing that first step?
◆ How can you avoid that?
◆ After doing that first step, what is another step you can take?

## The Cost of Overcommitting

Mismanagement of goal setting and emotional motivation to change can easily lead you to believe you can do more than you really can. You see this happen at work when people are trying to advance their career, so they take on additional projects that might completely overwhelm them. You also see this happen in people's personal lives where they might offer to hang out with each of their friends and help everyone with anything they need, leaving them little time to manage their own life. The result of overcommitting is generally the opposite of the original intent. Projects start to slip through the cracks, you mentally burn out, you can't keep up with all of your commitments, and your overall commitment to your mission is compromised or completely aborted. The stress and potential disappointment of letting yourself down can be a huge barrier for progress. But the real issue is not you letting yourself down but rather setting yourself up to fail in the first place.

One of my clients who wanted to lose 50 pounds originally committed to going to the gym six days a week for two hours. She also committed to completely cutting out all carbohydrates, as well as running a mile a day. She committed to going to the gym when it first opened at five in the morning, and before she could continue I had to stop and ask: "Is there an emergency that is requiring you to lose this weight in the next few days?" She laughed and told me no, but she just really wanted to commit this time. "This time?" I asked, "What do you mean?" She explained she had tried this many times before and "it never worked." I asked her what she had tried in the past that never worked and she described her exact commitments now only to reveal that when she did this in the past, she did everything she committed to for the first few weeks and then just kind of "fizzled out."

I see the symptoms of overcommitting—like fizzling out— all the time. And in part, that's due to attacking your desired change with just intensity instead of consistency.

Imagine you're going on a first date with someone. They drive to pick you up, and you're waiting anxiously to see what they have planned for your first-ever outing. They get out of the car and walk around the front of the car as if to open the door for you, but suddenly, they get down on one knee, hold out a ring and flowers and chocolates, and ask you to marry them, letting you know their mom is in the backseat as a surprise waiting to meet you so that you can start planning out the wedding.

That's not how you form a long-lasting commitment to some-one—if anything, that's how you get smacked with a restraining order. As ridiculous as that example sounds, that's what people do when they try to replace consistency with intensity. Instead of doing reasonable steps regularly and consistently improving over time, they sacrifice logic at the impulse of their patience so they can hopefully speed up the outcome. Inevitably, this is a counterintuitive approach because overcommitment usually results in very temporary action leading to burnout and recession. This is why in the program Alcoholics Anonymous members are encouraged not to make lofty commitments or pledges to "never ever drink again" but instead are encouraged to take it one day at a time. Breaking down missions into manageable everyday actions and committing to making effective decisions in the moment is a solid strategy to effect change.

You can't speed up consistency or time. You can't make unrealistic commitments that end up threatening your progress. You have to do the work, regularly, and not attempt to replace time's role in progress. You can gradually build on your commitments as you create this new habit. You can assess what commitments can be added to as you fulfill your obligation and responsibility to see them through.

A failed commitment was never a real commitment in the first place. You can't outwork a bad commitment.

One of my favorite sayings to my clients back in the day still rings true in the work I do now with people and organizations alike:

"I'd rather you be 80% on track for two years than 100% on track for two weeks."

Set yourself up to see progress by committing to the actions achievable today to move in the direction of your mission. A reasonable commitment is one that you can achieve consistently without negotiating or burning yourself out.

You need to intentionally reexamine the commitments you have that may be keeping you stuck so that you can disrupt them.

You need to intentionally reexamine the commitments you need to make that will help you change course for the better.

Managing your personal commitments is your job. It's your personal responsibility to commit to what betters you, and that responsibility is one of the most effective tools for change. There will always be a degree of dependence on yourself to be willing to help yourself. But dependence on self combined with getting help through accountability is another change tool you have at your disposal.

> "Dependent people need others to get what they want. Independent people can get what they want through their own effort. Interdependent people combine their own efforts with the efforts of others to achieve their greatest success."
>
> —*Stephen Covey*

## Communicate for Change

Approaching phase two of the Changing Course process, you probably see the danger of putting all your eggs in the individualistic basket for success. Hopefully, you recognize the need to own your habits and actions without shutting out the world and going it alone. That realization is vital for your next step in the process of navigating real change—and it requires you to speak up.

Two major contributors to effective change include communication and accountability. Both can motivate change to occur initially and encourage sustained change. But without communicating the problem that you plan on correcting, there is nothing to be held accountable for.

Your willingness to address the problem takes honesty and ownership. But your willingness to communicate that issue that might have plagued you deeply for a long time is more than just ownership—it's vulnerability. Similar to asking for assistance, vulnerability often gets incorrectly associated with weakness when, in actuality, vulnerability represents the strength to be seen as you are. Your willingness to commit to change and communicate a vulnerable part of yourself to someone else demonstrates strength. To communicate your real problems requires authenticity and courage to sidestep the anchors of change such as shame and perceived weakness. There is nothing embarrassing about being honest with yourself and someone you respect while asking for help. Communicating vulnerability creates a social and workplace environment that encourages openness and collaboration. Yes, it is much easier to share your wins and strengths. But it is much more effective to also share the areas you need help in that you are choosing to work on. People are not mind readers, though.

It may be in people's nature to help, but they can't help what is hidden from them.

In a perfect world, there would be this perfectly packaged, spontaneous help from someone that is so strangely specific to your situation that all your problems would vanish. Even kids' movies avoid that much fantasy. While it would be great if someone just offered you the help you needed, that's not usually going to happen.

Most of the time, assistance only happens after a request has been made. You have to communicate your needs. You have to ask for the help. How is your boss supposed to know you need help getting more comfortable with a specific process? How is your best friend supposed to know you are really struggling with being afraid to pursue an opportunity and you'd like their help? How are the people around you supposed to know you are committing to making a big change and want their support in the process?

Across multiple studies, direct requests to get assistance from peers made up more than 90% of all help encountered in different organizations.

Awareness is not the only barrier to someone else helping you. The people who are able and willing to help you need to know that you even want help, that you're open to their help, and how exactly you're hoping to get their help. From relationship settings to mentorship settings to even therapy and friends, without communicating the scope of the problem and their potential role, very few people will insert themselves into a situation they haven't been invited to. If you've ever put in a maintenance request of any kind at an apartment or with a private service, you have to actively communicate the problem and the details about the problem, as well as invite them to come take a look and potentially help.

"Hey, are you willing to help me out with something I've been struggling with?"

"Hey, would you be open to helping me with this issue I've had?"

"Hey, you are one of the few people I trust, and I really respect your advice. Are you open to helping me with this problem I've been dealing with?"

You don't need to sell them on helping you. You simply need to see whether they're willing or open to potentially helping you and possibly tell them why you chose them.

While you'll need to put in that specific maintenance request here, they won't be fixing your leak—just offering insights and accountability as you do the job that was only meant for you to do. That external accountability on top of your commitment and self-accountability just improves the odds of you seeing the changes you want to become your new normal.

## Improving the Odds

What do piano lessons, weekly team status meetings, and visits to health care providers have in common?

Accountability that encourages people to follow a specific course of action and contributes to the success of the mission.

Knowing you need to do something is not enough. Knowing you have someone to talk with and who's going to check in on your progress drives more actionable behavior.

The Association for Talent Development conducted a fascinating study about goal setting and accountability, and the results are pretty eye-opening. Here is a summary of what they found in terms of likelihood to complete a goal (based on the behavior you engage in):

- **Having an idea or goal:** 10%
- **Deciding that you will do it:** 25%
- **Deciding when you will do it:** 40%
- **Planning exactly how you will do it:** 50%
- **Committing to someone that you will do it:** 65%
- **Accountability appointment with someone you've committed to:** 95%

How often have you found yourself wanting or even telling yourself you "need" to change or act, yet nothing really gets done? If I had two thumbs, I'd be pointing them at myself because I've definitely been guilty of doing this.

Accountability really is just the act of communicating your problem and, because of that communication, holding yourself to account for your actions moving forward. The simplest acts of accountability, such as communicating your goals with friends and updating them regularly, contribute to a higher rate of success than those that don't.

That update could look something like this:

I know we always text each other TikTok videos of cats getting scared of cucumbers, but I'm really committing to putting myself out there by applying to at least 20 jobs a week and talking to recruiters on LinkedIn. I really want a job change so I can ultimately make a career change. I'm just letting you know what I'm committing to, so I'll check in regularly, but don't be afraid to see where I'm at if you're open to keeping me accountable!

Just putting your struggle and willingness to commit out there serves as a reminder to you that you're doing this and you owe it to yourself (and now your cucumber cat friends) to see your commitment through. In addition to telling your friends, sometimes it helps to designate one specific accountability partner that is more than a sounding board.

The ideal accountability partner is someone you respect and value. This could be a boss, coworker, friend, partner, therapist, or honestly even a stranger on the Internet. Their role really is going to depend on what they are willing to offer, but ultimately, it's the act of telling them your struggles and what you plan on doing about it with continual updates that's going to benefit you most. It isn't their job to make sure you do your work—that's all on you. They're there for you to voice your real problems and to remind you of the commitment you're making to change, whether directly or indirectly, just knowing you have to check in. Your decision to communicate to them your willingness to correct the real problem serves as your motivation to act. The motivation to act with urgency comes from knowing you committed yourself in front of someone you respect. You know you don't want to go back on your word. You know this is what you need. And you know next week, the only thing that separates a good accountability follow-up from a bad one is what you decide to do in the meantime.

On top of having an accountability partner, using different accountability devices will help motivate and sustain the changes you aim to make. An accountability device acts as a way to disrupt distracting forces not helping you achieve your commitments and trigger you to refocus. These could be anything from constant calendar invites to do specific tasks to which you committed to reminders on your phone to screen time limits on your phone and more—any method that reminds you frequently to accomplish the tasks you need to do today so that you remain accountable to changing the course you're on. Here are some of my favorites:

- Blocking off calendar times for specific tasks
- Placing sticky notes in high-visibility places (refrigerator, desk, mirror) with specific tasks
- Setting alarms and alerts to disrupt activities that I easily get lost in (social media, emails, negative news cycles, etc.)
- Using a Pomodoro timer (or crappy egg timer) for focused work

Now on the off chance you don't find an accountability partner, you can become your own partner if you genuinely make use of these accountability devices. Frequently reminding yourself of your goals and responsibilities and sharing them with people influences your commitment to act and adhere to your mission.

Let's compare strategies:

Person A: "I need to lose weight."

Person B: "I need to lose weight, so I've decided I will commit to walking 10,000 steps a day and track that with a cheap step counter. I will walk in bouts of 10 to 15 minutes multiple times a day. I've set three calendar reminders a day to go for a walk. Three days a week, I've blocked off 40 minutes to do a full-body workout routine from home that I found on YouTube. I wrote down my goal of losing 20 pounds this year and my commitment to all of these actions. I will review that screenshot of my commitment whenever I am feeling unmotivated or catch myself being distracted if the reminders don't do that for me."

Honestly, who do you think is more likely to take action and keep taking action? It's not about being hard-core or overcommitting to unrealistic expectations—it's about setting yourself up for success by disrupting patterns that might still exist that got you in trouble in the first place.

Adherence or continued decisions to remain faithful to your commitments is heavily influenced by accountability but not just any kind of accountability. Recall your parents telling you that you need to clean your room or you won't be able to watch TV. This may be a form of accountability, but it relies on controlled accountability where consequences and threats are used to encourage you to comply. Compare that to a more autonomous accountability that relies on internal desire to complete a task and make the accountability partner proud. The internally motivated accountability will create more sustained adherence over time, so it's important to want to change instead of just feeling forced to change under duress.

Think about a time when the owner or a higher-up plans on visiting your job, and you're aware of it. Everyone scrambles to clean the floors and be on their best behavior. Sometimes interactions are embellished unnaturally, following procedure by the book and loudly so they can hear you doing a good job. This kind of example of accountability is more short-term, but it serves as an example of the Hawthorne effect, which simply states that measuring or observing behavior changes behavior. You probably know that feeling of being on your best behavior because someone "important" is watching. It motivates you in a way to just make sure you're doing what's required of you to your best ability. But instead of just waiting for an owner of a business to scare you into cleaning your station, remember that you're the important person in your life coming to examine your current habits and actions. Measuring your own behavior will help you change it to align more with the outcomes you want and the potential you have.

Measures of accountability, accountability devices, and adherence are critical determinants of creating, motivating, and sustaining change. Others may help along the way, but that help is a bonus on top of your own personal commitment to act and hold yourself accountable.

Your growth is your responsibility. Make sure you don't play the victim or blame others for your role in keeping your commitments to yourself.

> "Take accountability . . . Blame is the water in which many dreams and relationships drown."
>
> —*Steve Maraboli*

After nearly two decades of putting my hand in a pocket or glove to hide my biggest insecurity, I finally decided to fix what I wasn't willing to face. I lied to myself for long enough saying things such as, "If people see my hand, they will never love or respect me" and "I'm just that guy with the glove. It's fine. It's a part of who I am." But I chose to stop lying and see the real issue—I was hiding from myself and didn't accept that I am good enough without hiding my hand. I communicated my willingness with my former partner as a way to reassure myself that I am making this commitment. I am obligating myself to stop hiding and choosing to hold myself accountable to taking the first terrifying step of taking my glove off as well as the following steps of adhering to accepting myself without hiding. It is so damn hard sometimes to let your guard down so that you can change the way you operate, regardless of the fact that what you're accustomed to might be hurting you more than helping you.

I led myself through the discomfort with honesty, ownership, and accountability. I was tired of falling back into the same old rut. I was tired of telling myself I "needed" to do something but never actually committing to changing. Communicating out loud what I kept inside all those years prompted me to take the leap most of us know we need to take.

You'll be forever grateful for taking personal responsibility in rerouting the course of your life. One small decision after another. One small commitment after another. One-degree different trajectory.

How can you take the issue you've brought from subconscious to conscious and communicate it now?

Let's say you're struggling with sales calls. Instead of staying on the rusty nail, how about telling your boss, "Hey, I'm struggling with these sales calls, but I'm committed to the process. Can you hold me accountable and/or offer any advice?"

In *The Wonderful Wizard of Oz,* the Lion lets the others know that he seeks courage. In doing so, he unknowingly takes ownership of his struggle and shares that vulnerability with Dorothy and the others. The lion is holding himself accountable and gets shared accountability from his group. He is validated, heard, and seemingly has a weight lifted just by sharing what he is struggling with.

It is easy to shy away from feeling the weight of the true problems you're facing. The honesty required to take ownership privately of that struggle is difficult, but nothing compares to letting go of your ego and sharing that hardship with those closest to you.

You'll never receive the advice you need from the struggles you fail to communicate.

Accountability does not need to be a rigid check-in process like hiring a personal trainer or talking to your boss (although that does work for some people). Accountability can simply come from knowing you turned that internal problem you normally sweep under the rug into a dirt pile out in the open for people to see. And if you're like most people, you will focus a little more on that pile in the middle of the floor now that you know someone may be coming over to check on you.

Communicating the issues you're struggling with can feel freeing and empowering. By publishing a YouTube video showing my hand, I exposed my dirt pile and threw away the paint can lid. I allowed people to see me with my disability.

As a result, people saw me, and I was free. I couldn't turn back even if I wanted to.

Make your realistic commitments that you can stick to on even a less-than-great day. You can always build on the success of those commitments through self-accountability and seeking help through accountability from others. The promises you keep to yourself alongside the commitments you are willing to uphold will make the accountability process simple. That accountability will serve as reminder that you are capable and committed to changing the course you are on for the better.

Now it's time to broadcast that change to the world (kind of).

---

## Stop and Think

◆ What past commitments might be holding you back?
◆ How can you disrupt those past commitments?
◆ What commitments can you 100% make to yourself today? This week?
◆ How will you hold yourself accountable in detail?
◆ Who might be some of your accountability partners?

---

People get obsessed with changing themselves for the better as long as that change does not involve actually addressing real problems.

The perpetual drive to be better is an avoidance of reality. How can you be a better version of someone you refuse to be in the first place? Better is not a place. More is not a place.

Are you subconsciously keeping yourself stuck by being in "working on yourself" mode instead of taking action? If so, you're in good company. People get stuck in external help—self-help books, therapy, motivational YouTube videos, positive podcasts—only to find themselves never actually progressing and just using all of that help as an alternative form of substance abuse.

I call this a toxic help cycle, where you're buffering, not trusting your own abilities and judgments. When you're in the toxic help cycle, you've shut down your endogenous production of self-belief and require exogenous assistance not to fix the problem but to stay alive. But this change process is truly up to you. You have to realize the dichotomy between not being broken and needing to commit to small action to live by example. The example you will live by can be read about day and night but will not come to life until you broadcast it.

**Dorothy:** I'm going to miss the way you used to holler for help before you found your courage.

**Lion:** Well—I would never've found it if it hadn't been for you.

# CHAPTER 8

# Step 3: Communicated to Broadcast

**KEY TASKS FROM THIS CHAPTER:**

- Separate your identity from your past habits.
- Decide what habits your ideal self would have.
- Model that behavior for yourself and others.
- Celebrate the small wins fast and frequently.

Judy Huemann contracted polio at 18 months old, taking her ability to walk and requiring her to use a wheelchair. At the time, in 1949, no one could have expected Judy to become "the mother of the disability rights movement." Legal protections for people with disabilities didn't exist yet, but systemic barriers did. At 5 years old, Judy was denied access to her elementary school, which declared her a "fire hazard" because of her wheelchair. Instead, all they could spare was two and a half hours of home education a week. Discrimination and exclusion didn't stop there for Judy. Neither did her determination to do something about it.

Even despite accessibility and societal barriers, Judy graduated college determined to become a teacher yet was denied her teaching license by the New York Board of Education. The grounds? Solely because she was in a wheelchair. Judy sued the board, winning the case to not only become the first teacher in

New York who used a wheelchair but mark a historical turning point toward the rights of people with disabilities.

Judy went on to marry Jorge Pineda, who also happened to be a wheelchair user, and together their love and partnership further dismantled the stigmas and tragedy attached to people with disabilities at the time. "Disability only becomes a tragedy when society fails to provide the things we need to lead our lives," Judy remarked, but not just for the sake of acknowledgment—she did something about it.

Judy went on to play a pivotal role in the development and adoption of key legal protections for people with disabilities such as the Americans with Disabilities Act, Section 504, The UN Convention on the Rights of Persons with Disabilities, and many more. Working alongside both the Clinton administration and the Obama administration, Judy really did change the world up until the moment she passed away.

> "Some people say that what I did changed the world but really, I simply refused to accept what I was told about who I could be. And I was willing to make a fuss about it."
>
> —*Judy Huemann*

Are you prepared to live out the life your current habits are creating for you?

By now, you've made big strides in acknowledging and communicating something that you were uncomfortable to even face before. You've recognized the ineffective language models you used previously that contributed to your staying stuck. You've identified the root problem. You've given yourself a prescription to change, and you're committing to holding yourself accountable through realistic and consistent actionable steps. You've communicated your willingness to others as a way to motivate yourself to change as well as get outside help and accountability from others.

Do you realize how big of a deal that is? I'm not one for participation trophies, but it has taken me over two decades to do all this, so if you are accomplishing everything I mentioned so far, take note of your accomplishment. While the reward generally comes after the work, I'm a big believer in celebrating the work as it's done. Whether the success is building a million-dollar enterprise or committing to working out or holding yourself accountable to rebuilding your confidence, that deserves recognition from you.

Countless people quit. Too many. For a variety of different reasons—some more valid than others. But quitting is not relevant to you as you've done this process thus far and made it here. Bravo.

Now it's time for the final step of the Changing Course process, taking your problem from communicated to broadcast. This is what I consider the "larger than life" step. It's time to take the thing that you struggle with most and actively live by example, turning your active commitment into action that also acts as a tool to help others.

The true key to changing yourself is understanding this one simple concept, a concept that states that you really can't change yourself at all.

## Identity Protection

This entire book is about change. Recognizing a need for it. Planning it. Committing to it. Creating it. Sustaining it. Motivating it. But just understand, I'm not really asking you to change yourself—just your habits. I've always been me. Judy has always been Judy. Dorothy has always been Dorothy. You have always been you. These truisms tell us something about change: It's more about changing your habits than it is about changing who you are. And in separating your identity from your actions you give yourself a chance to focus on the possible (changing your habits) as opposed to changing who you are (I'm not even sure what that really means).

By chance, are you a morning person? For so long, I told myself, "I am *not* a morning person." I didn't do well getting up before 10 a.m. Even though I was a gym person, I just preferred later workouts and later days. If anything, I was a night owl. Whether you are a morning person or a night owl, you are actually just attaching your identity to your current habits, making your claim effectively untrue.

I wasn't a night owl—I just had a habit of going to bed late.

I'm not a gym person—I just have a habit of going to the gym.

You are not a morning person—you just have a habit of getting up early.

You will always be you. You are the constant or permanency in your life. But your choices, habits, and beliefs can change at any time. Without getting into a philosophical debate on what the self is or isn't, let's acknowledge how great it is that you are not a prisoner of your past habits. Any attempt to create a permanent, fixed identity based on habits you can change at any time is an ineffective strategy that reduces your actual capacity for change.

Changing course requires you to correct your language and beliefs so that you stop viewing your habits as an extension of your identity.

It's easy to attach your identity to your current or past habits, though. The danger of identifying with your habits is developing a fixed mindset on that partial truth. You begin to believe you are or are not something at your core, which influences your beliefs and choices. You take what you see without fact-checking, allowing your brain to pass judgment and negatively influence you.

One of my favorite accounts on Instagram is @goob_u2 run by John Dorsey. John, who has a law degree from the University of Pittsburgh, uses his platform to maintain ethical standards of transparency mainly in the fitness industry. Simply put, he puts influencers who lie and Photoshop their bodies in efforts to manipulate clients into buying their programs on blast. His account focuses on accountability, honesty, and transparency (and it's hilariously entertaining). Why, though? Because manipulating the truth and letting half-truths go unchecked creates unrealistic beliefs that ultimately hurt people. He does his part to correct that. And just like @goob_u2, you have to do that in your own life.

Don't let yourself be manipulated by changeable habits to believe you are stuck. Anyone would get stuck if they were told by themselves and everyone around them what is possible. Believing that who you are limits what you can do is the epitome of learned helplessness or conditioning yourself to believe something is unchangeable (even if it is). There is no real future if your current abilities are limited to your past habits.

Instead of saying, "I'm not an organized person," tell yourself, "I have a habit of not prioritizing organization."

Instead of saying, "I'm not a gym person," tell yourself, "I have a habit of not going to the gym."

Instead of saying, "I'm not a timely person," tell yourself, "I have a habit of not being on time."

Instead of saying, "I'm not a confident person," tell yourself, "I have a habit of not feeling confident."

By removing the identity masking the habits that can be changed (if you want them to), you restore your power to course correct. More important, you have the freedom to untether yourself from who you used to be to make room for who you want to be.

The ideal version of you recognizes the habits you need to distance yourself from and the habits you need to implement. And the ideal version of you is the same exact person you already are—it's the "you" who untangles identity from habit and chooses to live by example.

## Stop and Think

- ◆ What habits of yours have you attached to your identity?
- ◆ When have those false identities influenced your thoughts and choices?
- ◆ How might separating your habits from your identity make change easier?
- ◆ What benefits come from not repeating your ineffective habits of the past?

## Live by Example

For me, initially, communicating my insecurity around hiding my hand was extremely public. I had to separate my habit of hiding my hand from the identity I took on of "I'm just not someone who shows their hand." The leap took the form of a YouTube video that subsequently went viral. That step I thought would be the hardest for me—the first move. But broadcasting my continued real self was a different kind of hard. I had to learn to live by example.

You're probably familiar with the phrase "lead by example," but this last phase doesn't stop at leading. Living by example means upholding your commitments to address the real problems—from language and insecurity to avoidance and fear—not once or twice or intermittently but every damn day. To do this effectively, though, you have to create habits and behaviors that reflect your ideal self. Your ideal self is just another way of saying the version of you that is more curious than certain.

"Let go of certainty. The opposite isn't uncertainty. It's openness, curiosity and a willingness to embrace paradox, rather than choose up sides. The ultimate challenge is to accept ourselves exactly as we are, but never stop trying to learn and grow."

—*Tony Schwartz*

## Changeless Certainty

Think back to a time when certainty failed you. The employer you were certain you'd work for forever let you go. The relationship you were certain was the one didn't pan out. The plant you were certain you could keep alive is now dust. We often overestimate our certainty in situations for the wrong reasons.

Certainty might not be about knowledge and confidence as much as it is about preserving our internal beliefs about who we are and our limited view of the world. It's less about evidence and truth and more about what we want to be true to maintain internal consistency (remember my discussion of cognitive dissonance in Chapter 2).

Ludwig Wittgenstein, arguably one of the greatest philosophers on certainty (I'm certain), ironically noted in his book titled *On Certainty* that "the difficulty is to realize the groundlessness of our believing": nothing holds it up from "underneath"; rather, other beliefs of ours "hold it up from the side," per se (like a web). The "groundlessness" he refers to is the lack of factual information we use to create "certainty." Our assuredness is held up "from the side," meaning we reach and cherry-pick our information, manipulating whatever we can to create our truth all the while avoiding the truth.

When you rationalize certainty, you can create comfortable lies that double as change blockers when the reality of uncertainty hits. Recall a time where you were sure you couldn't do something, yet you somehow did it: asking for a raise, hitting a personal record, finishing a seemingly hopeless project, finding a way out of a "hopeless" situation. In fact, everything you were certain would kill you or destroy you or stop you from moving forward was untrue—you made it through. Maybe with battle scars and maybe with a lot of adapting, but that certainty now seems pretty unreliable. Instead of operating from a sense of certainty in how you need to do things, how you need to think, and what can be done in situations, the much more effective choice leading to your ideal self is operating out of a sense of curiosity.

## Get Curious

You know those times when curiosity gets the best of you and you end up accidentally inventing the microwave? No? Well, Percy Spencer was an engineer working on a radar project for Raytheon, the defense company. Percy noticed the chocolate bar he had in his pocket melted from the heat so he got curious. He put popcorn kernels and then an egg near the equipment and he confirmed his curious idea that the heat generated from microwave energy could cook food. He went on to develop the microwave, which has become a staple in many homes and hotels worldwide. Now, my curiosity in this regard may have only enticed me to put Peeps (those duck-shaped marshmallows) in the microwave until they exploded, but curiosity has helped me much more than that.

I took my glove off after 17 years one time in a video and communicated my real problem of shame and self-consciousness. But now I need to live with my glove off? Doing something hard once is difficult enough, but damn, now I need to relive that hardship every single day. I didn't know if I could do that. I started to tell myself certainties that "I couldn't do it" and "I need more time." Ineffective language can spout at any point you find yourself in unknown waters just like it did for me, so don't forget what you learned in Chapter 3. But instead of listening to the false certainty, I leaned into the curiosity: "How can I do this? How can I make this easier on myself? What steps can I take that would help? What can I use to combat the resistance? Why am I assuming I have to do everything all at once? Do I really need to take an "all-or-nothing" approach?

Transitioning your certainties into curious questions in the face of difficult decisions prompts you to look for solutions

**Table 8.1** Certainty Statements versus Curiosity Questions

| Certainty statements | Curiosity questions |
|---|---|
| "This isn't going to work." | "How can I make this work?" |
| "This is hopeless." | "How can I navigate this effectively?" |
| "I can't do anything." | "What are all of my options here?" |
| "I've tried everything." | "What could I do better now?" |
| "I'm stuck, and I have no options." | "How could I start to get unstuck?" |
| "I'm screwed." | "What can I actually do in this situation?" |

instead of giving up. You want to focus on open-ended questions that give you a different vantage point of all the possibilities—not just the possibilities you may be programmed to favor. Table 8.1 shows what that transition can look like when you go to use this strategy.

Using all the skills you've learned in this book, you can live by example by filtering out ineffective language and certainties and reframing your situations with more of a "How can I?" approach. In doing so, you can make forward progress incrementally despite your former habits leading you to calling it quits.

The "How can I?" approach requires more than just curiosity for solutions—it requires you to adapt.

## The Imaginary Box

Curiosity breeds adaptability that makes room for outside-the-box thinking and options that might not be as apparent when you are too zoomed into the problem. Take the nine-dot exercise in Figure 8.1. Using only four straight lines, connect all the dots (and be sure not to lift your pen). Give it your best shot to solve it. Some people can solve this exercise using just three lines; absolute mastery would allow you to solve it using one single line.

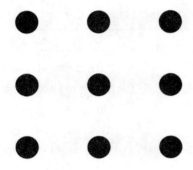

**The nine-dot exercise:** Using only four straight lines, connect all the dots *without* lifting your pen off the paper.

Figure 8.1 The nine-dot exercise.

If you're anywhere near as stumped as I was, don't feel bad at all. This exercise is meant to open your mind to how we sometimes weigh ourselves down with limits and rules that don't necessarily exist. This is a creative problem-solving exercise aimed at helping you expand your beliefs and possibilities so you can broadcast your ideal self as you learn to live by example.

As you see the variety of solutions in Figures 8.2, 8.3, and 8.4, you might be tempted to say, "Well, I didn't know I could go outside the box!" My simple response to you would be this: "What box?"

There is no box. There never was. Your mind created a limiting belief by simply seeing the situation and creating "rules" to solve the problem. You probably couldn't solve the problem because of your rules—rules that never existed—yet you believed them and operated as if they were true. You box yourself in when you create tight parameters on how you can solve problems. That often creates more resistance and risk of failing to meet your commitments.

You commit to going to the gym three days a week, but something happens and the gym is closed one of those days. You also happen to be traveling another one of those days.

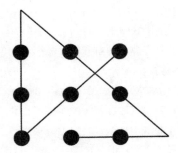

One possible four-line solution.

**Figure 8.2  A possible four-line solution.**

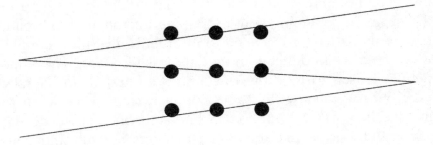

One possible three-line solution.

**Figure 8.3  A possible three-line solution.**

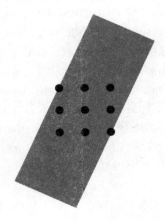

One possible one-line solution.

**Figure 8.4  A possible one-line solution.**

The certainty mindset will steer you away from your goal, telling you that you can't work out two of those days, but curiosity will encourage you to ask, "How can I?" You then realize the real issue wasn't going to the gym but just working out. You can work out anywhere: a park, a hotel, at your house, or anywhere. Even if you don't have weights, you have options: gallons of water, pots and pans, siblings you love, children, grocery bags, suitcases full of money (I'm kidding—no one has siblings they love). You can always adapt if you're open to being a little more curious as to how.

Going back to being sure I couldn't tolerate people seeing my hand, not only *could* I tolerate it, but I did. It was harder in the beginning, I'll admit, but every time I committed to broadcasting the behavior I needed to in order to live my example, it got a little less difficult and a little less terrifying. The same people I used to hide my insecurities around (read: literally everyone) were now the same people watching me learn to live life in a way I'd hope to inspire someone else to do the same. But how could something that terrified me and controlled my life for years become so easy? Was it just me or can this work for anyone?

Evgeny Sokolov, a Russian neuroscience researcher, formulated the early concept of habituation, which can explain how broadcasting your new behaviors gets less difficult over time and consistency. Habituation refers to a lessening response to a repetitive stimulus. Prolonged and repeated exposure creates an adaptation to no longer eliciting a response from the subject. It's a form of learning in which with frequent exposure comes a weakened response that eventually can turn into no response at all. Once you become habituated to a stimulus, it can also diminish the strength of response to similar stimuli as well.

The moment I decided to never hide my hand again, I had to actually stop hiding my hand (stimulus). At first, I would have severe anxiety and tense up every time I showed my hand in public (response). But over time, my mind adapted from struggling to show my hand to being okay with it to barely noticing it to never having my hand be a second thought. That process made me feel, "Well, damn, if I did *that,* I can do any-thing," and my confidence started to shine both outwardly and inwardly. People began perceiving me as confident, but more important, I started feeling confident in myself and my capacity to keep growing.

This phase is all about leaning into your stimulus by taking action. The temporary discomfort of new action becomes a regular part of your everyday life over time. You will learn to adapt to this foreign action and temporarily uncomfortable response if you maintain your efforts.

Habituation is change—change in the way you feel, respond, and live by example.

In moving from communicated to broadcast, you become the person you wish you had as a real-life role model when you were going through your own worst experiences. But how do you become that real-life role model instantly?

You don't. You simply pick actions that you're willing to commit to aimed at solving your real issues:

**If you decided to be the *best* possible version of your-self today ...**

How would you start the day?

How would you handle negative internal dialogs?

How would you handle some of the work you've been avoiding?

How would you handle needing a new job or career path?

How would you handle improving your health?

How would you keep your commitments to yourself?

How would you begin your process of changing course?

Consult the best version of yourself and use that person's way in every part of your day. The best version of you is just you making better decisions. It isn't some unrealistic superhero or business mogul or leadership guru who lives in the foothills of the Himalayas. The best version of you is you right now, from this point forward. You now live according to that standard without negotiation or compromise. If you need to make 10 more sales calls, make those 10 calls instead of avoiding them. If you need to get back to the gym but you're afraid of starting, remember both habituation and having an accountability partner will only make this process better. Each passing time you prove to yourself you can do this, you broadcast your best self.

This phase is not to be taken as a nonstop exhaustion phase of constantly being perfect and high energy and acting like Gandhi when someone pisses you off.

Remember, you don't become your best self overnight. You are learning by doing repeatedly, building the skill of linguistic programing that leads to better thoughts, beliefs, and actions. You identify the real issue at hand and own up to your role in it. You communicate your commitment of changing course to hold yourself accountable. And you broadcast your new action as you set and accomplish realistic tasks repeatedly and consistently as you progress.

## One Hundred Percent Effort, Not Perfection

Now, I'm not a sports guy, but I know basketball players practice all the time, countless hours a day. They don't go into practice or games saying, "If I miss any shots, I'm done. I quit." But they also don't gently parent their way out of giving 100% effort.

One hundred ten percent effort is too much, and 99% effort is too little.

If that statement rubs you the wrong way, you need to understand why.

"Ninety-nine percent effort is not too little! It's much more than I usually give!"

As people, we tend to be more tolerant of our own shortcomings and stricter and more judgmental of others. Your struggles are not your shortcomings, though—your reasoning to give less effort than you can is. Relativity is a sinister method of enabling subpar choices. It can be used to validate suboptimal choices that stop you from choosing the best course of action. Poor past mistakes are not an excuse to make slightly fewer poor mistakes when the possibility for optimal choices is present. This can be seen in all walks of life, including but not limited to lifestyle habits, relationships, and personal decisions in general.

Jon is heavily addicted to opioids. On average, he takes four times the recommended amount that he gets from his drug dealer. He eventually goes to rehab and has the ability to completely get off drugs. Instead, based on relativity, he doesn't really need to quit as long as he does less and maybe gets a prescription.

If Jon had a choice between getting the support he needed and fully quitting or just using much less than he usually does, which should Jon choose? Well, Jon has a choice. And that choice, albeit a hard choice that I can empathize with, should not be disempowered by relativity when Jon could be utilizing his full capacity.

Here's another example: Jennifer has a really crappy boyfriend who treats her poorly. She "upgrades" to a moderately crappy boyfriend who still doesn't treat her how she wants to be treated, but she validates this choice by thinking, "He's better than my last boyfriend."

Don't justify making a relatively better choice when you have the capacity to make an optimal choice.

One hundred percent effort is what you can always give relative to what you have, and that is exactly enough to get yourself unstuck and change the course of your life.

Don't get me wrong; Energy and capacity fluctuate. On days when you are sick or have less energy or for whatever reason have a limited capacity, you can still give 100% of what you have available to you. The person who gives 30/30 is living by example, whereas the person who gives 70/100 made a choice to give less effort, reducing their bond to give what they can to create change. That's why it's so important to build on small habits and choices every day as you learn to live by example. You create evidence that you can put 100 percent effort into a small task consistently. You then curiously ask yourself, "If I can do this, what else can I do?" Your confidence in yourself grows as you start stacking up all these small wins. And if you really want to sustain this new way of life, broadcasting your best habits to yourself and those around you, you have to learn to celebrate fast and celebrate often.

## Clapping for Change

Whether you're building a winning culture in an organization, in team sports, or in your own personal life, celebration is the glue that binds motivation, action, and consistency together. When you were a kid, your parents might have celebrated every little thing you did, from putting your toys away to using the toilet for the first time. Parents do this to help instill habits and behaviors through positive reinforcement—tying action to a good feeling and praise. Acknowledging wins reminds you of your accomplishments, but it can seem awkward to celebrate small wins. I mean, are we really going to celebrate correcting a bad thought the same way you would celebrate finishing a marathon? Absolutely.

While finishing a marathon is an incredible accomplishment and deserves to be celebrated, so does the act of completing your first training session a year earlier. Big wins like that are often the result of compounding small wins over time. The sooner you can link a positive feeling to a new action you took to live by example, the greater the probability of that action sticking and becoming automatic. As you celebrate your daily wins, you might have less champagne and paparazzi, but you have an equal opportunity to credit yourself for the work you're actively doing. The celebration piece also serves as a way to measure progress and own the wins, as well as areas of opportunity to win next time. Again, it's not about participation trophies but about not ignoring your completed commitments as you are changing course.

Let's say you tend to isolate yourself and struggle connecting with people. You recognize the root is confidence and self-belief, so you begin correcting your internal dialogue. Every time you catch limiting thoughts, you swap them for effective thoughts. And you celebrate those moments, wiring your brain to welcome this new habit often. As your language changes, you build confidence to commit to meeting one new person a week with a simple conversation but just slightly more than, "Hey." You strike up conversation with someone at your favorite bookstore and surprisingly talk for 15 minutes. After you celebrate your commitment and ability and reflect curiously, "If I can do that, and that wasn't so bad at all, what else can I do?" You now catch yourself isolating much less as time alone becomes more in your control when you want rather than accept that it is who you are.

Small commitments. Small actions. Frequent celebrations. Repeating this process helps create and sustain change by motivating you with a sense of accomplishment, tying happy emotions to new behaviors to help them stick. Sometimes those commitments will be bigger. Sometimes those actions will be bigger, too. Your capacity for what you can honestly handle will fluctuate, but celebrating your wins is nonnegotiable (Fogg 2019).

Winning bias happens when someone who wins believes they can keep on winning, so they inevitably keep on winning.

You probably recall phrases in and out of sports or games such as "They're in the zone." Those noticeable moments of repeated success can spill over into all areas of your life. Win enough moments to notice a streak where that streak becomes a pattern and then a belief, and you'll set yourself up to win for life. You've had many wins in life already. The problem is you didn't remember them or celebrate them enough.

Living by example involves winning and winning often. But you can't win often if you don't set yourself up to win consistently. And you can't win consistently if the action isn't truly achievable. Most important, you can't achieve if you don't act.

Celebrate that sales call you made.
Celebrate going to the gym when you didn't feel like it.
Celebrate organizing your desk every day before work.
Celebrate speaking to yourself fairly.
Celebrate taking the first step.
Celebrate taking the fifth step.
Celebrate every day you give 100% effort.
Celebrate every commitment you keep to yourself.
Celebrate every bad habit you stop from happening.

That celebration evokes positive emotion that fuels motivation to keep going, which reciprocates into more positive emotion and motivation. Celebrating your desired actions is your cheat code to sustaining behavior change while positioning you to pursue more of what you want, asking yourself, "What else might I be able to win at?"

Reinforcing your own growth is not the only benefit of broadcasting your new habits, though. That broadcast isn't just influencing you but also the world around you (whether you know it or not).

## Lighthouse

The pros outweigh the cons of making these changes for yourself. Unlocking the version of yourself who filters out assumptions and half-truths from your life leaves you real chances and opportunities to get and stay unstuck. You have a chance to live in a way that not only benefits you but teaches people around you how to live by example, too. This broadcast phase provides a new sense of external motivation to keep growing through your own issues—not just for you but for them.

Leaders and people alike underestimate their influence on other people. You have been modeling behavior both intentionally and unintentionally since you were born. You learn not only from what educators, parents, and bosses teach you directly but also from what they show you in their own way. Effectively, everyone broadcasts how they manage life, which can lead to the people around them learning vicariously through their examples.

Social media and social media trends are a form of social behavior modeling. People are influenced to adopt trends of certain users especially when they see those users gaining followers or getting a ton of views and likes. People also follow celebrities, influencers, and other creators, and over time, they might start dressing differently, forming different opinions, and changing certain parts of their behaviors or beliefs.

Even in the workplace, you learn to adopt behaviors of those who are more successful or at least those who stay out of trouble. Unfortunately, modeling behavior works both ways, though.

If all of your friends normalize drugs, irresponsibility, or a lack of drive in life, you're at higher risk to join them by following their behavior. Leaders are not omitted from the negative side of modeling, either. It doesn't matter how much a leader tries to teach their staff values of respect and time management if they are constantly late or distracted with other tasks during meetings. Regardless of what they say, people see behavior and are influenced by your actions.

You may not desire to be the next viral dancing influencer, but regardless, you are influencing people currently. The way you choose to communicate, solve problems, and hold yourself accountable acts as a lighthouse for others around you. For some, that influence may be small, but for others who choose to follow your behavior, ask yourself this: Is your lighthouse leading people to the rocks or to the shore?

Historically, racial segregation, discrimination, and an overall lack of civil rights has plagued the United States. The 20th century, though, was a time of change and struggle against discrimination, marking efforts toward inclusion and civil rights. Some prominent figures in history broadcasted their beliefs through simply living by example. Their choices to be vulnerable and authentic without negotiating their commitments to self and society influenced the way we experience the world now.

In 1908, William English Walling wrote an article about a race riot that killed seven and ended that article by broadcasting an appeal for readers to come to the aid of the Black community. Mary White Ovington read that article and answered the call for action. Even though her own community would have likely shunned her decisions to support the Black community as a white person, she went on to help establish the NAACP.

In 1955, Rosa Parks broadcast to just a bus full of people by not leaving her seat. Her action sparked a historic flashpoint for change.

Through the 1980s, 1990s, and still to this day, Oprah Winfrey inspired many—especially girls—in the Black community, by owning her power and showing what is possible for a woman to accomplish.

When Martin Luther King, Jr., went off script and broadcast his dream at the March on Washington in 1963, his words became an anchor of the civil rights movement.

Fred Rogers, a popular white television host, regularly used his children's TV show, *Mister Rogers' Neighborhood,* as a platform to broadcast his views on challenging societal issues, including but not limited to racism, police, and more important, respect, understanding, and equality. There was one particular episode, in May 1969, when he chatted with his friend Officer Clemmons, a Black police officer (unheard of, with the bad relationship between the Black community and police) and shared a small plastic wading pool with him (unheard of in 1969) to cool off their feet.

All of these people were role models. All of these people broadcast their best selves even in some of the worst times. Change requires unwavering commitment and willingness to be a lighthouse for yourself and others. And a lighthouse doesn't stop broadcasting its light in the darkness of a storm—that's when it is needed most.

These people were role models. And so are you. You became a role model the day you were born. Like it or not, by being born you become a lighthouse for others. Your parents, your employees, your partner—everyone in your life gets influenced by you, to some degree.

Imagine if we all lived with this awareness! How much good we could do in the world if we were behaving as if we were role models.

This is why the old adage of "Do as I say, not as I do" is so important. Parents, bosses—humans of all kinds—love to give advice that they don't follow themselves. Hypocrisy and inconsistency not only confuse people watching you but also build a false sense of progress for yourself. Giving advice does not mean you don't take the advice yourself. Where you set no consistent example, there is no good leadership or influence.

If a parent tells their kids to clean up their toys but throws their own personal stuff all over the house in an untidy manner, the kid will be confused and maybe even refuse to adopt the seemingly unfair behavior that isn't reciprocated.

The same goes for a leader to their employees. You cannot reasonably ask of others what you aren't willing to do yourself, within the lines of your job role. The CEO might not make 300 sales calls a day because that's not their role. But I have met a CEO who epitomized leading by example and being a role model for everyone in the company. The late Tony Hsieh, former CEO of Zappos, was known for his unique (and sometimes bizarre) antics when it came to leadership, culture, and service.

I was fortunate enough to have been involved with Zappos when they put on an adaptive clothing fashion show where all the models had some sort of disability. This was my first time really showing off a part of me that used to cause me so much discomfort, yet I found myself strutting my stuff down the runway in Las Vegas rocking Nike adaptive shoes called Nike Flyease that had a patented zipper technology, making it easier to take them on and off.

I loved the shoes, clothes, message, and everything Zappos had to offer and quickly grew close with their upper management. Much to my surprise, there was a Zappos All Hands meeting across the street where every major brand Zappos worked with had their C-suite executives attending. I was pulled aside, because they knew I was starting my speaking career, and asked if I'd like to speak on stage in between runway shows.

I excitedly accepted and headed backstage to get mic'd up. That's where I met Tony. His energy was incredible, and he immediately took an interest in getting to know me. Billions of dollars sat in the crowd representing these brands and, at that time, I probably had a whopping $393 in my bank account. Yet he gave me his undivided attention. He made me feel valued, important, and that I could conquer the speaking world. And I did just that over the years. I really wish I could thank him. I was just unaware that that would be the last time I'd speak to him before he passed away.

Not only did Tony have a huge impact on me; he had a massive impact on the world. He scaled Zappos to a billion-dollar company yet never lost the philosophy that service to his employees and customers comes first. Living the culture you want comes first. He had the same kind of desk the newer salespeople had. He often worked among his employees. He encouraged creativity and service, which ultimately led to one of their many successful side quests, Zappos Adaptive, which serviced people with disabilities in the adaptive apparel space.

Tony led by example. He was a lighthouse of a leader who inspired others to become leaders. Tony broadcast his successes and shortcomings with authenticity replacing conventional authority and connectedness replacing commandments.

One of the steps in both Alcoholics Anonymous and Narcotics Anonymous is to remove yourself from your environment. That's because people have power and influence over other people and act as role models for them, by default. If getting away from people because they're bad role models is a step for these programs, that tells us something. And that something is that people have power.

When you recognize that your behavior becomes a lighthouse for other people, you tend to discover a newfound sense of responsibility.

Where is your influence leading people?

Is your broadcast helping people or hurting people?

How does what you say align with what you do?

Are you being the person you wish you had growing up?

Be the person who shows others that it's possible to get unstuck and solve the problem they're struggling with. Be proof for others that they can get through what you've gone through.

If you don't take your problem from conscious to communicated, or from communicated to broadcast, you're teaching people that it's fine to keep going down the path that's keeping them stuck and in pain. That it's fine to break commitments to yourself. That accepting the reality of possibility is less important than accepting the limiting beliefs we create ourselves.

I'm not sure about you, but knowing that I can potentially help people just by living like my ideal self would is a huge source of motivation to broadcast my best out there. This is the transcendence from self to others, which is weird because I don't believe in altruism.

Everything is selfish. And that is not necessarily a bad thing. Try and name one thing that's not selfish as in something you like to do solely for other people. Volunteering? Helping someone? People-pleasing? Charity? Philanthropy? All of these (aside from people-pleasing) are great, and all of them give you something in return. You feel good or happy that you could help. There is reciprocal satisfaction you get in helping, and that is okay! Helping others is a form of prosocial behavior, or just intent to help others.

The benefit to prosocial behavior is you get the nice feeling that comes along with being an awesome role model. Plus, you get to continue being the best unstuck version of yourself.

Another way to think about being a role model is to consider your behavior as an act of indirect reciprocity. If we all promoted cooperative behavior and fostered strong communities, others would be encouraged to join in, without expecting something in return. It would just be understood that by doing a good deed, that good deed might be reciprocated one day.

There is a payoff beyond your life being better that includes the feelings you get for being a role model for other people. Don't believe me? Go to the gas station, spend 15 minutes there, and open the door for people. You instantly feel better by keeping the door open for someone. For me, personally, doing kind things for other people holds me accountable and encourages me to lead by example.

The broadcast piece of the Changing Course process becomes the sustainability of change.

Building a lighthouse is not a one-and-done exercise. You have to man that thing all the time. Through your willingness to live by example, manning that lighthouse becomes automatic, like breathing or telling the waiter, "I hated it" after you ate your food really fast.

You might be reading this book because you have a specific change you want to make or because you want to get better at managing change.

Change management is language management.
Change management is accountability management.
Change management is habit management.

But I want you to understand this is not a "set it and forget it" situation. It's a revolving door.

You have to live this to maintain it. You have to be in this continually. The life that you live in this place can still be stressful—in your organization, in your home, and in your head. Things still happen. Change happens. You will probably screw up, or be screwed with, and that will create more problems.

When that happens, go back to Step 1.

Life is basically a game of Chutes and Ladders. It's up and down, down and up, and it is definitely not perfectly linear. Getting to the top of one mountain doesn't place you at the peak of all mountains.

Change as a whole is overwhelming. But we have our sights on a one-degree shift to change course.

## One-Degree Shift

Sitting down the first time with a therapist, I didn't know what to expect. As we talked, I told her how overwhelmed I was setting all of these goals and how I couldn't perfect the things

I was taking on, so I avoided them. I hated the idea that I could go on stage or write a book or teach workshops and not be the best speaker or author they've ever heard. I told her I take on a lot all the time but really just want to be the best I can be.

She looked at me quizzically and said, "Who told you you had to be the best? Why do you need to be so special? Why can't you just be good or average?"

I didn't really have an answer. But it made me think of all the impossible pressure I put on myself to be "special" and do all of it with perfection all at once. She asked me, "Is enough enough for you?" to which I resisted the urge to lie and told her the truth: "No."

My brain hijacked my sense of what enough is. I had come to believe I needed to be the best and do more. That anxious desire to be more than enough led me to taking on too much and burning out or defeating myself mentally before I even started.

We get our own way by setting ridiculous demands on what we need to do and why. While I want to progress and improve, I don't need to be perfect to start. I just need to start. I needed to build confidence in the idea that small action that sticks is better than large action that sinks.

You can get better and do more with time. You cannot be the best and do it all right now.

As you continue the Changing Course process, adapt the mindset of making just a one-degree difference. A flight from Los Angeles, California, to Milan, Italy, is about 12 hours. But if that airplane shifts just one degree north or south of that direct path, you could end up in Austria or even Tunisia. On a similar note, if you had a lone penny and doubled it daily, by the 15th day you'd have $163.84 and by day 30 you'd have a whopping $5,368,709.12. The effect of compounding small changes over time can be enormous.

Don't underestimate the big benefits of changing course by just one degree or 1%.

Saving $8.25 a day = $3,000 a year

Walking 5,000 steps a day = 33 marathons a year

Reading 10 pages a day = 15 books a year

Meeting 1 new person a week = 52 potential new
                                    acquaintances per year

The perfect outcome we want can be overwhelming, which is why the one-degree difference approach helps you gradually get there without being overwhelmed and potential resistance.

If I had to write down everything it would take for you to lose 50 pounds, it would look completely exhausting, explaining everything from calculating your basal metabolic rate with the Mifflen St. Joer equation to figure out your total daily energy expenditure by adding an activity multiplier and then instructing you on how to take that total calorie goal and break it up into macronutrient goals of carbs, which have four calories per gram, protein, which has four calories per gram, and fat, which has nine calories per gram. And we still aren't even 80% of the way through what needs to be done!

If I told you that you'd have to take 55,000 steps to complete a marathon, that would also seem exhausting. But whether it's 55,000 steps or 550,000 steps, it comes down to the compound effect of one step repeated. Just like a painted room is the result of the compound effect of painting one wall and one wall is the compound effect of one paint stroke.

The Scarecrow, the Tin Man, and the Lion reaching Oz were the compound effect of Dorothy taking one step forward. In *The Wonderful Wizard of Oz,* each character took their problem from subconscious to conscious. Then they communicated what they needed and broadcast what they learned in Emerald City.

It can be hard for people to change on their own. But when they communicate their problems with others, it can become much easier to get to the heart of the issue and to change.

The Dead Sea and the Sea of Galilee are both fed by the Jordan River. The Dead Sea is dead because it has no outlet for all the salt, making it impossible for aquatic life and vegetation to live, let alone thrive. The Sea of Galilee does have an outlet; it broadcasts—and in it lives lush vegetation and thriving marine life.

> "As we work to create light for others, we naturally light our own way."
>
> —*Mary Anne Radmacher*

If you don't live as a role model, what are you adding to humanity? Whether your humanity is your team leaders, your employees, your friends, family—anyone and everyone who sees how you operate in the world—you're teaching them something.

Great role models make the world a better place when they live by example. If they don't broadcast their positive shift, they're just like the Dead Sea.

The Changing Course process can be used for just any issue you face in life, from personal to professional and everything in between.

From general emotional overload and uncertainty on exactly what is wrong to feeling stuck in a particular area in your life, this process will help you gain clarity in the real issues so you can make your one-degree difference toward initiating and sustaining change you want.

You might not have verbalized this yet, but you know you have to do something. Take the issue through the Changing Course process. Let's use relationship change as an example. Start by writing it down and taking your problem from subconscious to conscious. What do you perceive is wrong with the current relationship dynamic? Use the Five Whys technique to find the root problem. What would you want it to be? If you had a daughter, what would you want her relationship to look like? Does yours mirror that ideal? Putting pen to paper and taking ownership of the issue is your first step.

Once you've identified the problem, reach out to the person you trust most in the world and be honest with them about what you're struggling with. External parties aren't wrapped up in the same emotions as you. They can think more rationally, and from a different vantage point particularly when it comes to romantic relationships. By moving from conscious to communicated, you're able to expand your perspective on the issue and start to develop commitments and accountability for actions you plan on taking. The commitments and way you choose to broadcast your ideal self through living by example are an extremely personal and individual choice. My ideal self and your ideal self are uniquely different. I cannot tell you what to do. All I can hope to do is give you a process and framework to effectively navigate your personal choices to change.

If your love life is thriving, maybe you're having issues at work. You keep going back and forth between whether you're going to quit or wait until you get fired. Either way, something's not great in your career. When you start writing things down, you might realize that your core issue is that you don't believe you're good enough to excel in your role or that you hate the industry you're in.

While this might be a crappy realization, it's actually a gift. You can't fix what you're not willing to face. What actions can you take to feel more successful at work? Adopt the "How can I?"

mentality. Get curious and think outside the box for potential solutions. Be willing to take small steps to get unstuck, and hold yourself accountable to those small actions. Make achievable personal commitments to yourself.

Could you set up five sales calls a day? Six? Ten? Can you rope in one of your teammates and communicate your insecurities and goals to them? Ask whether they'll be willing to be your accountability partner. Operate how your best self would with every objection and wave of motivation. And don't forget to celebrate the wins—not just the sales but upheld promises you made to yourself and how that makes you feel. Freeze those new habits as you continue, and recognize your change may be inspiring others to do the same. Those effective habits will stack through the curiosity of "What else can I accomplish?" and sooner or later you can mentor someone who was in your exact shoes when you first started.

The beautiful thing here is that you end up with a story to tell others. You weren't happy with your performance, so you reached out for help, and now you're closing more sales and winning business because you're holding yourself accountable.

Suddenly, you're broadcasting that to others so they know what resources exist and don't have to go through the same stress that you did.

## Your Yellow Brick Road

We all hope for an Oz. We want some powerful, all-knowing wizard to step in when change hits us hardest to save us from the struggles and work we'd otherwise have to do ourselves. Dorothy and friends had high hopes to meet Oz and have all of their needs met, only to find out the all-powerful wizard was just an ordinary man hiding behind the curtain of illusion. Maybe you're like me and relate to hiding behind something like a curtain, mask, or in my case, glove. Looking back, it's sad that someone might feel the need to pretend to be something they are not, thinking being themselves simply wasn't enough. What Dorothy and the gang realized is they had the ability to get unstuck and manage their change the entire time, they just needed to find their yellow brick road and get some support along the way.

I hope that this book can serve as part of your Yellow Brick Road, but I know your process and journey will be different than everyone else's.

During your change journey—whatever your Yellow Brick Road looks like—don't wait for an Oz to save you. Don't lie to yourself about your courage, ability, or limited situation. You have everything you need right now to take one step in the ideal direction.

Don't wait for Dorothy to come and show you the way. Be Dorothy.

**Dorothy:** Home! ... I'm not going to leave here ever, ever again ... there's no place like home!

# CHAPTER 9

# Real–World Application

The COVID-19 pandemic has taken the lives of millions of people and unarguably caused mass hysteria, distress, and turmoil financially, physically, and emotionally. But pandemics are not a modern-day phenomenon. The term "pandemic" was coined in 1666, but pandemics can be traced back as far as 430 BCE from the Athenian Plague to the Black Death in 1346 CE to the Spanish flu in 1918. Add on HIV/AIDS, Ebola, and SARS, and you see that history naturally has experienced pandemics not as a rarity but as a natural phenomenon. All pandemics can lead to both short-term and long-term economic harm.

The similarities or normalities of pandemics are what is most fascinating. Our most recent pandemic being the last widespread and rapidly spreading virus was the first pandemic of its kind after antibiotic discovery in the 1940s. Even with our medical advancements since then, the process and reactions to pandemics were comparable from the black plague to the Spanish flu all the way through COVID-19.

Scapegoating (i.e. finding someone or something to blame) is seen with almost all pandemics. During the cholera outbreak in the 1800s, riots happened because people believed "elites with physicians as their agents had invented the disease to cull populations of the poor" (Cohn 2018). During the same outbreak, in Russia, physicians were blamed for poisoning the wells, resulting in the targeting of medical staff. During the SARS pandemic, the Chinese accused Westerners of poisoning their wells. And for COVID-19, China along with political parties, pharmaceutical companies, anti-maskers, and elites have all been blamed.

Time and time again, governments have been caught suppressing the news from minimizing severity and ignoring beginning stages to full suppression of death tolls. At the start of the Spanish flu while World War I was still active, the chief medical officer of the British Local Government Board made a point to claim that it was "unpatriotic" to be concerned with the flu rather than the war. That flu ended up killing 50 million people.

Anti-mask coalitions were also formed in different pandemics, including the Spanish flu in the early 1900s, quoting some officials discussing the unconstitutional nature of mandating masks in an attempt to control the masses where one official in Portland even said, "Under no circumstances will I be muzzled like a hydrophobic dog."

From public distrust and social distress to scapegoating and loss, history has shown that it is not out of the ordinary for sociopolitical disturbances to be paired with pandemics. And pandemics are a very ordinary part of existence.

**Life is change.**

There's no such thing as normal as a baseline. Zoom in close enough, and you can use the confirmation bias to mark any good stint in life as normal. Zoom out far enough, and you'll see every kind of event possible happens at different points in time. If anything, change is normal as it is one of the few constants.

So if life is change and change is normal, it's fair to say that life and all that happens within it is normal. Chasing those glimpses of "normal" is like chasing a mirage. It doesn't exist. Disasters, pandemics, and setbacks are all part of the deal of being alive. Luckily, history is a testament to our ability to adapt.

Humans have survived everything from the First Agricultural Revolution to the advent of AI, and we've evolved.

You hear people lamenting about the "good old days." But which "old days" are we talking about? When we go on about how the 1980s were simpler, we're neglecting to remember the awful things that were going on in the world then. It wasn't just about neon and big hair. In the 1980s, AIDS was a death sentence and considered a "gay disease" by the president. Video began to kill the radio star. There was a severe global economic recession. Casual racism, sexism, and homophobia ran wild. The Americans with Disabilities Act had not yet been created. Yes, you can cherry-pick your ideal scenario, but instead of cherry-picking a time that no longer exists with a false narrative, why not pick the time you're currently in and make it a reality?

The pandemic was awful for many reasons. But it was not out of the ordinary. Life happens, which means pandemics happen, loss happens, struggle happens, happiness happens, success happens, and death happens. What you really mean when you say, "I wish things would go back to normal" is, "I wish things would go back to benefiting me most."

Life is an ongoing story. Fixating on one chapter doesn't do us any good. Besides, you only have your perspective on how that chapter went.

Here are a few examples of how we have been navigating change—forever:

### ◆ The Agricultural Revolution

Humans advanced (which is debatable) from being nomadic hunter-gatherers to settling into communities and growing food. This change gave our ancestors more control over the amount of food they had available.

We can assume there were cave people who didn't think farming would work. How do you manage insects and deal with unpredictable weather patterns? There were probably many who wished they could go back to hunting lions and tigers and bears (oh my), but, fair enough, that was before donuts were invented.

◆ **The Industrial Revolution (Late 18th Century–Early 19th Century)**

When machines and factories took over the work of human artisans, people started moving from rural areas to urban ones. Production became more efficient, and there were more goods available.

While paving the way for Amazon and Walmart, we lost many traditional crafts, and many artisans lost their livelihoods.

◆ **The Automobile Industry (Early 20th Century–Present Time)**

Humans needed a more efficient way to get themselves to work and to the shopping mall than horse-drawn carriages.

But while automobile manufacturers enjoyed exponential growth, carriage makers became obsolete.

◆ **The Rise of Electricity (Late 19th Century–Early 20th Century)**

While most of us can probably agree that electricity was a damn good invention, think about the companies that would have gone out of business when things like gas and oil lamps became unnecessary once we had light bulbs.

◆ **Digital Media (Late 20th Century–Early 21st Century)**

We're living through a time in history when newspapers and traditional print are becoming irrelevant. Chances are you're not even reading this book on paper. We love the convenience of having access to information on demand, but a lot of companies can't and won't survive this transition.

Not to mention, e-commerce has significantly disrupted the brick-and-mortar model. Give us our Amazon Prime, but what has the cost been for hundreds of small businesses that can't/won't compete?

I could go on for days. Cable has become a dinosaur thanks to streaming services.

Nobody has a landline phone anymore, in favor of smartphones. Bank tellers and grocery store cashiers have been replaced by self-serve options, etc.

However you choose to look at it, life will have macro- and micro-transition periods. Accepting change allows you to understand the true meaning of the all too repeated phrase "moments that will last a lifetime." That is, moments are temporarily yours while the memories of those moments are permanently yours.

This transition period for you may be changing the course of your life for one reason or another. Up until now, I've provided stories, frameworks, and concepts for changing, but I also believe real-world applications are vital to see the process in action.

Below are three core areas of your life with examples to help you navigate change and get unstuck using the Changing Course process. The following case studies and scenarios are based on actual accounts of people and organizations I've worked with. Names and key identifying features have been removed for privacy purposes.

## Health

Jon is 37 years old and planning to get married to his beautiful wife-to-be next year. This huge event in his life has triggered a desire to achieve a goal he is still unsure can even happen— lose 40 pounds. Jon has always been known as "the hefty guy," though. He asks himself the Five Whys to find out what he is truly struggling with: He does not believe he can do it as he has always quit in the past.

Jon has taken his subconscious struggle and made it conscious. Using more effective language, Jon is able to separate his identity from his habits, understanding who he has been is not who he has to be. He makes a commitment to himself that he will start with a 20-minute walk every day and only eat fast food twice a week. He tells his best friend his commitments and asks if they can check in weekly before their normal poker night.

Knowing he has a check-in weekly, Jon begins completing his commitments. Every week, Jon proves to himself he can do this, celebrating his wins with his friend and his partner. His motivation is increasing so he decides to go to a gym twice a week as well.

A few weeks later, Jon is regularly going to the gym and walks every day if he can. He naturally doesn't choose fast food anymore and has lost almost 11 pounds. More important, Jon has made this his new normal, and people notice. His other poker buddies start asking what he is doing, and now they are walking and being more active, following Jon's example.

Seeing the progress, promises kept, and positive influences he has on others, Jon maintains this behavior to not only hit his goal for the wedding but also to become known at poker as "Jon the fitness guy." Jon is just Jon living by example.

## Wealth

Jess is 46 years old and a mother of two boys, one 18 years old and the other 20 years old. She has dedicated her life to her kids, being the best possible mom she could, even though she still feels that she could've done more. She makes enough money to get by but is now for the first time questioning whether this is what she wants to do for the rest of her life or is it just "too late" to change. Jess puts effort into discovering that she is afraid of the unknown because she needs the illusion of control. This has made Jess shy away from taking risks.

Jess starts asking curious questions to see what she would do if she wasn't afraid of uncertainty. It turns out Jess has always wanted to start a business online. Adopting the "How can I?" approach, she lays out a creative way to maintain her current job for security while putting five hours a week into learning about building an e-commerce business. Jess tells a colleague she respects that she is committing to learning five hours a week, and they meet every Monday to go over her progress.

As she is learning, she is realizing it is not half as scary as she thought. She didn't need to drop everything and invest everything. Little steps. She slowly acquires an LLC and then has a friend help her with a basic logo and website design. She celebrates these wins and finally goes live. In the first three weeks, she gets two sales, one being her aunt.

She remembers change is not immediate and uses outside of the box thinking to try different marketing strategies. Idea number seven creates a little buzz, and Jess has her first 30-order day. Jess celebrates and learns from this. Jess continues for over a year, getting to the point where she could supplement her normal income if she wanted. Others start asking Jess whether she could teach them what she learned. She helps a few friends and starts putting out free advice on YouTube, and suddenly her channel and store start racking up views and customers. Jess played what most people call the long game but in reality, it's just the game. And she hasn't won but rather chooses to win every day.

## Relationships

Nadine has been faithful in her relationship for five years. After being high school sweethearts, she and her partner followed the so-called normal steps of dating, moving in together, and considering marriage. While they have had many good moments, Nadine can't help but feel something is missing. While the beginning of their relationship was fun and exciting and came so naturally, over time, Nadine has felt that her efforts are the only efforts that exist anymore. Nadine is not sure what to do, so she starts the Changing Course process.

Allowing herself to explore and discover the real root of the issues, she realizes she feels she and her partner are just going through the motions of a relationship and life in general. She doesn't like the feeling of just existing in close proximity to someone she loves. She questions what could have led to this situation and ultimately uses the Five Whys technique to discover they both have just given more time to work and quick dopamine hits such as TV shows and social media than they've given to each other.

Nadine takes her subconscious-to-conscious findings to a therapist to communicate what she is thinking and feeling. She hopes for a little accountability in the process of trying to better her relationship. Nadine makes her own commitments to communicate more effectively to her partner, as well as make her own efforts to value her partner instead of waiting for them to take the lead. She also decides to communicate to her partner what she is feeling in a healthy way to explore a way forward together. Through Nadine's vulnerability and communication, her partner recognizes and acknowledges they dropped the ball with making each other a priority. Instead of Nadine taking a knee-jerk feeling and misconstruing the situation in a negative light, she uses curiosity instead of certainty to explore what she can do about it.

Nadine lives by example and acts as the partner she wants. This, along with the direct communication, inspires her partner to follow that behavior, ultimately improving their quality of life inside and outside of their relationship. Nadine realizes they never lost love for each other; they just lost focus, and the compound effect slowly but heavily weighed on their relationship. Luckily, they just needed a one-degree shift in the right direction to get them back on track.

*****

The world isn't out to get us. It just keeps spinning and doing its own thing. Our job is to navigate through the changes that occur, not to get hung up on the idea that something not normal is bad. It's easy to get complacent or go on autopilot in certain areas of your life just to get through all of the duties, responsibilities, chores, jobs, tasks, and overall requirements of being an adult. It feels hard enough sometimes just to drive inside the lines of life carefully to avoid disaster.

But managing change isn't just about avoiding disasters. It's about steering your life in the direction you want it to go. Even the incredible technology of self-driving cars won't take you anywhere if you don't first decide where you want to go.

With no direction, you're just left stuck. But it's not just people in their personal lives who are susceptible to getting stuck.

Organizations, too, pay high prices for not innovating and keeping up with the rapid evolution of modern-day business.

## Factors That Keep Organizations Stuck

### RESISTANCE TO CHANGE
When companies are committed to the old way they've done things, change management is almost impossible.

Avon was known for its direct sales business model, where sales reps went door-to-door, selling cosmetics and other household items to their neighbors. Online shopping became a more convenient way to buy the types of things Avon sold. If Avon had embraced the Internet, they would have been in an ideal position to scale, helping them serve their loyal customers in the 100+ companies they had a foothold in. But they were slow to change and lost significant market share.

### LACK OF VISION OR STRATEGY
Organizations can stay stuck when they don't have a clear vision or a well-defined strategy. Radio Shack was once *the* go-to destination for tech toys and electronics. But they didn't have

a strategy for evolving to the world of online retail, which is pretty ironic when you think about it.

Radio Shack remained committed to its small stores with their out-of-date inventory, becoming obsolete, while giants such as Amazon and Best Buy offered better selection, more convenience, and lower prices. Radio Shack went bankrupt not due to a bad product or service. They simply lacked vision.

## BUREAUCRACY AND HIERARCHY

Organizations with rigid structures and outdated systems aren't exactly agile. With the rapid expansion of technology combined with companies competitively moving the needle to be more sustainable, more innovative, and more service-based, there is no room for organizations to be anything but agile.

In our personal lives, staying stuck can create a lower quality of life and take time from you, but when it comes to organizations staying stuck, even for just a bit too long compared to their competitors, they risk losing market share or worse—closing their doors on their customers and employees, who rely on that income, forever.

Blockbuster is an example of a brand that suffered partly due to a strict hierarchy. Between slow decision-making and failing to keep up with emerging trends, their structure and response time played a part in their demise. If they'd been more willing to shake things up from within, they might have survived the streaming era.

## RISK AVERSION

Some organizations remain stuck because they're too scared to take risks and innovate. Leading brands aren't immune to this. Kodak was hesitant to move away from traditional film to digital photography. Even though Kodak invented the first digital camera back in 1975, they were afraid to risk the success they'd built on film. They did eventually shift to digital, but it was too late. They could no longer compete, and they lost at their own game.

## COMPLACENCY (THE SUCCESS TRAP)

In some cases, a leading company doesn't feel any urgency to change because they feel secure in their past success. Despite having invented the OG mobile device, Research in Motion, the makers of the BlackBerry, failed to adapt to the smartphone market, even when the iPhone entered the scene in 2007. The BlackBerry's success made them complacent. They didn't embrace touchscreen technology and apps—the things consumers wanted.

They aren't the only ones, though. Seemingly unstoppable businesses such as Toys R Us, Sears, and many other department stores failed to adjust to the changing digital landscape, contributing to the downfall of multimillion-dollar businesses.

Sometimes complacency can even project a warped sense of reality that keeps organizations stuck (even if they don't recognize that they are stuck). It's hard not to circle back to Blockbuster here. The Motley Fool, an investing service and forum, interviewed the former DVD rental giant's CEO Jim Keyes in 2008 about the rapidly emerging Netflix and Redbox competitors. Keyes dismissively replied, "Neither Redbox nor Netflix are even on the radar screen in terms of competition." Keyes discredited the likelihood of being able to stream reliably and change the way people experience entertainment. That resistance to and avoidance of change really bit Blockbuster in the ass. Roughly two years later, Blockbuster went bankrupt.

To Keyes's credit, it is easier to know what we know now and ridicule him as opposed to him experiencing high levels of success reaching billions of dollars a year in DVD rentals (not to mention a whopping $800 million in late fees alone in a single year). This just serves as an important reminder that even on the best course of action possible, over time, if you don't adjust, you will undoubtedly run ashore.

**Dorothy:** What am I going to do about Miss Gulch?
**Hunk:** Now lookit, Dorothy, you ain't using your head about Miss Gulch. Think you didn't have any brains at all.
**Dorothy:** I have so got brains.
**Hunk:** Well, why don't you use them? When you come home, don't go by Miss Gulch's place. Then Toto won't get in her garden, and you won't get in no trouble. See?

# CHAPTER 10

## Accepting Feedback (without Letting It Defeat You)

When you think 100-year-old rugged outdoorsmen and construction worker products, the colors teal and hot pink probably don't come to mind. William Stanley invented a steel vacuum sealed container in 1913 for the likes of workmen, outdoorsmen, and adventurers to use from time to time. The company was already successful, but it wasn't until a few of their female customers noticed a large gap in their marketing strategy that they recently skyrocketed to the number-one hydration container on the market.

Linley Hutchinson, cofounder of online shopping blog The Buy Guide along with Ashlee LeSueur and Taylor Cannon, noticed Stanley had a quencher cup that was amazing and stylish for simply carrying cold water around all day. They heavily recommended this cup to their predominantly women demographic in 2017 but found that the cups were harder to come by and not exactly positioned, in their marketing, for women (like at all).

They reached out to Stanley about these cups to potentially work with them to better position the product in a separate market in 2019, but Stanley at the time didn't do any sort of real affiliate marketing. Instead, Stanley offered to wholesale 10,000 of the cups to their blog. The three founders took a chance and purchased the cups that Stanley deemed not a priority in their product offerings, and much to their surprise, they sold all 10,000 in less than five days (5,000 of them sold in an hour).

This led to a sit-down with The Buy Guide founders and the Stanley team. "We just sat down with the executive team and were like, 'You're marketing this cup to the wrong people,'" Linley said. Later in that meeting, Ashley followed with, "Stanley had been a company only producing occasional-use items. They were making items for people's camping trips or tailgating. We told them that this cup was a daily-use item. It was an everyday, all-day item. And that it needed to look good in people's homes and kitchens, with their outfits, and not just in the great outdoors."

Stanley, while seemingly set in their process as they had achieved great success already, established this partnership and took The Buy Guide founders' advice of appealing to women with different colors and user-generated content for women by women. This shift both directly and indirectly led to taking yearly profits from $73 million in 2019 to $750 million by 2023. Today, over 700 million people have used the hashtag #stanley-tumbler, creating an entirely new market for a fortified century-old company. The willingness to listen paid off bigtime.

It's easy to be stuck in your ways. I mean, you've survived everything thus far, right? Can't be too bad, right? In the months, years, or decades that you've been experiencing your problem, you've built an emotional wall around it. And sometimes that wall stops even you from seeing what's on the other side.

You've validated, protected, and buried it in an attempt to keep it hidden forever. As you should be aware from unearthing the real issues from subconscious to conscious, it is not exactly easy to be honest with yourself while working through all of that resistance. It's definitely not easy to act on correcting the issues you now have to face. The communicated portion establishes some accountability for you, and below, I talk about how to get the most out of that. I just have to reaffirm that no amount of accountability will make up for your personal responsibility and role you have to play to create change. Just as therapy and mentorship are not simply a person to report to or a system to follow, your communication for accountability is the acknowledgment that you are ready and willing to take action as well as ownership of that action and its outcomes, both positive and negative. By moving forward with this step, you are committing to not only do the work but also be honest with yourself and your accountability partner on how it's going without sugarcoating it.

When you start communicating and broadcasting your problems to others, their reaction is possibly going to be starkly different from how you perceive it. They don't have the same emotional tie you do, so they're going to call it out in a way that might come across as mean or dismissive. They may even have a different preferred style of helping than you, so it is important to remember that they are not you. It is unfair to hold someone else to a standard you keep for yourself, and it's definitely unfair to expect them to give you the exact response you want. Don't rely on hoping they read your mind and act as you would, as that creates unfair expectations that most likely will not be met. So instead of aiming to have them mirror you, communicate your needs and preferences clearly.

When I first stopped hiding my hand, some people said things such as, "Finally! You should have done that a long time ago!" or "The only disability is a bad mindset." Not helpful, reductive, and just annoying, honestly.

Imagine sitting down with someone you care about and confiding in them that you're going to start taking better care of yourself by eating better and exercising. What if they say, "Yeah, sure. I've heard that before."

Accountability in the wrong direction is not going to help you. You may have to show people how to support you. If you're aware that this may be the case, you can strategically prompt people to tailor their reaction before you divulge your problem.

What do you need from them? Do you need them to lead with empathy and kindness while not sacrificing the truth and accountability? Being validated is important, but confusing validation with excusing responsibility is irresponsible. Rescuing someone from honesty robs them of growth. On the other side of the same coin, there is no place for brutal honesty as brutality is completely unnecessary. Maybe you like the more hardcore approach of speaking in a language that is less based in feelings and more logical and blunt. Regardless of your preference, it has to be communicated when establishing the communication and accountability you want from them.

Setting the tone with your person by saying something to the effect of, "I really want to make this change. I know I've tried in the past, but it would really help if you could hold me accountable without being condescending or harsh." The right person will hear you out and your needs and offer their support in a way that best helps you.

We ask for support without saying what will help us in the process. If you don't know what you need, though, consider what might screw you over. What can someone say that would hurt you and stop you in your tracks? Berating your past, repeating your mistakes, visible snarky doubtful looks on their face (yeah, don't go to this person) all can have a negative effect on your outcome. It will be up to you to properly distinguish between negative criticism and honest account that might feel like an attack when in actuality, it's just uncomfortable to face those deep truths.

If you're asking for help, tell people how they can help you and how they can harm you. Change rarely presents itself without friction. If you can ride the momentum past that friction, you're golden. The more you can do to remove resistance, the more likely you are to achieve and sustain change.

When you have the attention of someone you respect and want to communicate your problem to—whether that's a friend, family member, mentor, or perhaps even someone you have developed a relationship with through social media—tell them what you need from them.

Be honest about where you are in your process of grappling with the problem, and set some boundaries around what you need. For example, you could say, "I have come to you because I trust you and think you could really help me with something I'm working through. That said, this process is fairly new to me, and the way I need help right now probably looks a bit different from how you might naturally give it to me. If you're open to it, I would really appreciate it if you could be mindful of asking questions rather than making statements as I tell you what I need to say." This helps you get the response you need, and it also guides the person and makes it easier for them to say the right thing.

Sometimes, even with a bit of coaching, the other person will say something that makes you take offense or feel uncomfortable. When this happens, give yourself permission to acknowledge that crappy feeling, but don't give yourself permission to quit because of it. If I returned home after every time I hit a speed bump, I'd never make it out of my parking garage.

Think about marathon runners completing a race. They don't beat themselves up and feel guilty when they pause for a banana and water. They recognize that doing so is a critical step of getting to the finish line. The same is true as you make your problem public and perfect the art of changing course.

Lean into the discomfort because it means you are making an active change in your life and putting in the effort to address something you very recently weren't able to even admit to yourself. With every uncomfortable moment, you are getting closer to actively living life the way you want instead of passively living life the way you've always done it.

If you don't have someone who can keep you accountable, find someone. Maybe that's going to be social media, a boss, an employee, a therapist. Just find someone you value. And once you find that person, you have to be willing to not swat things away that you claim to already know.

Every year, people set the same big New Year's resolutions: Lose weight, quit smoking, read more, and the list goes on. And every year a majority of those goals are not reached. It is not a lack of knowledge. You know you shouldn't eat fried food all the time. You know you should go to the gym. You know you shouldn't stop at the gas station to buy cigarettes. You know you should make time to read.

Knowing is not the problem. Doing is the problem.

Knowing is not enough. Oftentimes, when I'm talking to people about things they need to be doing differently, they say, "I know. I know." Stop saying that. It does nothing but make you look negligent in your own improvement. Reminding someone that "you know" but you didn't do anything is worse than just not knowing at all. It means you are fully aware of the problem but chose to ignore it.

In truth, if you really knew what to do, you would probably be doing it. Be willing to listen. Don't acknowledge that you know what to do. Acknowledge that you're doing it.

Knowing is not enough. It has to become an action. And your accountability partners are there to remind you to do that action. That is how accountability works.

The Winged Monkeys tearing Scarecrow apart.

**Scarecrow:** Help! Help! Help! Help! Help!

**Tin Man:** Oh! Well, what happened to you?

**Scarecrow:** They tore my legs off, and they threw them over there! Then they took my chest out, and they threw it over there!

**Tin Man:** Well, that's you all over.

**Lion:** They sure knocked the stuffings out of you, didn't they?

# CHAPTER 11

# Overcoming Pitfalls

This mission was clear: Sail to Ithaca. The process, well, not so much.

Homer's epic *The Odyssey* depicts a tireless and cunning Odysseus in his attempt to return to his home and wife after fighting for nearly a decade in the Trojan War. This deceptively simple task of sailing home evolves into 10 years of turmoil, presenting trial after trial for Odysseus and his crew.

Undoubtedly brave, strong, and clever, Odysseus like many feels victim to his brazen impulsiveness, pride, and arrogance. His bigheadedness led him to expose his name to Cyclopes, Poseidon's son, after taking his only eye. Poseidon's wrath ensued.

Despite warning and risk, Odysseus let his pride and arrogance guide his leadership time and time again, leading to dire consequences for his crew, ships, and length of his journey home. He tried blaming his crew and the gods, just resulting in further setbacks and hardship.

On this journey, Odysseus began to learn self-control and acceptance as he recognized his arrogant ostentatiousness was just resulting in delays and suffering. From taking goddess Circe's advice about the sirens' hypnotic singing to learning to accept what cannot be changed, Odysseus undergoes a gradual character development leading to a more humble, intentional person and leader, allowing his eventual return to his home, reclaiming his throne. The journey makes *The Odyssey* a timeless, classic representation of the hero's journey, but how much of that journey was merely consequences and pitfalls of poor choices? A lesson we see characters in stories often learn yet we are resistant to accepting ourselves: The mission is simple. The process is not.

Similar to Odysseus, each character in *The Wonderful Wizard of Oz* was challenged in multiple ways. Tornadoes, flying houses and monkeys, witches, Toto ran away over and over. All of these are pitfalls or potential blockades to the mission.

Pitfalls create discomfort by veering off the intended plan, whether by choice or force. They inevitably happen, so just like precautionary measures of having a spare tire, a first aid kit, and battery cables, you should be prepared to deal with the possibility of deviation. You do not have to have a pessimistic outlook and expect the worst, but you also should not live in a naive fairytale. Instead of expecting the worst, just don't expect perfection. Being open to the possibility of a pitfall positions you much better to deal with it than the person who is either overly negative and creates a pitfall through self-fulfilling prophecy or overly positive and doesn't even have a spare tire.

So what do you do when things change? When situations that keep you most comfortable change, what do you do?

There are always going to be moments to quit. Moments to quit are also moments to keep going. It's important to acknowledge all your options, not just the knee-jerk irrational ones.

Sometimes where you're going isn't leading you down your best path. You have to have the adaptation and willingness to change course. It's not going on a different course that's challenging. It's leaving the current course that's a struggle. The answer you thought you were seeking isn't the one you needed.

I remember being over the bridge on a Sunday afternoon just across the intercoastal from my house. I saw the bridge go up to let a few boats pass, and traffic was building up fast. I had one opportunity to turn around before the point of no return. The current route I was on would have me home in five minutes. If I turned around, it would take 15 minutes to get home. My mission was to get home (and eat that half of bundt cake I had left). My plan was to go over the bridge like I always did. Something seemed off, so I changed my plan and turned around. It took me 17 minutes to get home. Much less efficient. Much longer than anticipated. Until I realized my first plan would've resulted in me waiting for almost an hour as the Fort Lauderdale boat parade was taking place.

Sometimes we incorrectly commit to the plan or initial process instead of the overarching mission. Don't get me wrong, having a plan is vital to your success as long as it is constantly updated and flexible with the unknown unknowns of life. A concrete plan in a river of unknown possibilities sinks.

Your mission is your enduring purpose that generally remains constant. Your process is just your methods you use to get there. Methods change with new information, new environments, and new obstacles.

For so long I thought my mission was to speak for the rest of my life. I love speaking on stages, weaving concepts and solutions into stories to deliver outcomes for organizations and people alike. But what if one day I lost my voice? If the normality of disease chose me and it affected my ability to speak, is my mission finished?

No, I could still write. I could still express myself. I could still help others. This made me understand my true mission: Help people and organizations see their world without limits.

Speaking is just a part of that process right now and hopefully for a long time.

An unwavering mission gives rise to innovation and adaptability. An unwavering process gives rise to stagnation and lack of optimization.

How many times have you caught yourself committing to a path, process, or procedure that you know is inefficient, yet you do it anyway? A plan is only as good as your ability to recognize when it needs to change. Commit to the overall mission, not the process.

Many pitfalls come from committing to the process more than the mission. If you're trying to lose weight, you might go to the gym five days a week and step up your running regimen, and then you hurt your ankle. When this happens, most people stop eating well, stop going to the gym, and stop doing everything because of a pitfall messing up the plan.

But there are hand bikes and upper body machines. There is still lettuce; you don't have to eat donuts. There is so much more that you can do. The option to fail presents the option to change course—to modify the process to maintain the mission.

Most people don't see the option to change course; they see the option of changing course as a failure. Nobody gets through life without pitfalls. Your pitfall is a different pitfall for someone else.

One thing that's constant is that change happens, and one day you find out that you're not in Kansas anymore (metaphorically speaking, as you may very well be in Kansas).

There are people who say things such as, "It's easy for them but not me."

People put this kind of thing out there to make themselves feel better.

"You're so lucky."

People distance themselves from solving the problems that hurt them.

We seek comfort and safety. Staying stuck is safe. You can't fail if you stay stuck. If you only fail once, that's less pain than failing multiple times. Failing is riskier to the brain than managing the failure you're already comfortable with.

**The lizard brain is not responsible for our quality of life. It's only responsible for our survival.** And that is a major pitfall to progress.

You have to override that lizard part of your brain and say, "Thanks for keeping me safe, but the way you're suggesting we do this is not allowing me to live my life." Acknowledge the safety mechanism, but don't abide by it. Don't live your life according to staying safe. A car is safe in a garage, but it never drives. And a car is meant to drive.

The best way to avoid problems is to not do anything. How much are you going to live as a reductionist in your life so you don't have to face the problem?

Safety is important to humans, but safety decreases your quality of life over time if you focus on safety alone. It's not a this or that thing. It's a combination. But people like to live in a this or that world.

I want to be an entrepreneur, but I don't want risk.

I want to be a better leader, but I don't want self-improvement.

I want to change the course of my life, but I don't want to read this book (ha).

This is all real life. I've struggled with it, too. And when I find myself feeling stuck, I go back to the Changing Course process.

You very well might get stuck in the process of wanting to change. Whether it's writing things down or talking to people and never moving out of the phase you find most comforting. It feels good to check things off our list and feel that we're making progress, but I want to make sure you know some of the common pitfalls so you can recognize them when they happen.

If you are able to see issues in advance, you can fix them before they derail you.

## Pitfall 1: You Buy the Book but Don't Implement the Process Fully

Just because you already know you need to do the work doesn't mean you are immune to this pitfall. If you go to the gym three times in a year, nothing is going to happen. Same thing if you go but do the exercises incorrectly.

This book is either your guide to change the course of your life or one of many books you say, "I'll read it *eventually*."

Having a therapist doesn't mean you are healing.

Having a library card doesn't mean you're studying.

Having a gym membership doesn't mean you're training.

Having a copy of this book doesn't mean you're changing.

Just because you're present doesn't mean you did what you needed to do. Just because you bought this book doesn't mean you completed the process. Don't confuse the success of the moment for the success of the mission.

In 17th-centaury Japan, *tsundoku* was a term created to describe a tendency to buy books but never read them. The intention to read them is there, but you never quite get around to it. It is not necessarily a bad or good thing. Just a description of a common behavior that I myself have definitely done. The big issue here is that this book specifically is meant to get you unstuck. It's meant to help you and maybe even your family or organization change course. And that can't happen if you don't read this book in its entirety.

It is a common pitfall when trying to achieve something that people focus on immediate gratification actions that call for little effort or time:

Get healthy → Buy new sneakers and fitness accessories

Learn photography → Buy the best camera and equipment

Read more → Buy a kindle and audible membership

Change course → Buy this book

Shopping gives you a nice dopamine hit as it provides instant gratification. "You created a goal and acted on it—great job!" your brain says to you. If you're human like me, you know there's a solid chance the only real action you'll take is opening those packages, flip through your purchases, and put them away, somehow forgetting that you ever got them.

Too often that dopamine release acts as a substitution to actually doing the less fun work. You don't need new shoes to stop eating unhealthy foods. You don't need the best equipment to learn photography. You don't need more books if you haven't read the other ones you have.

Most important, you don't need to buy this book if you don't plan on doing the stuff in it.

The pitfall is thinking that the easy purchase will solve the problem for you. Getting the thing only matters if you use the thing to achieve your intended goal.

Use this book to navigate change (and not just for its pop of color on your shelf).

## Pitfall 2: You Let the Illusion of a Simple Process Make You Think It's Going to Be Easy

The Changing Course process is a three-step process with a three-part tool. That's it. Because of its simplicity, you might trick yourself into thinking that it's going to be pain-free and easy. The people who acknowledge that they're going to be uncomfortable through this process are those who are going to benefit most from it.

If change were easy, I promise you this would've been an email, not a book.

What you're about to do is going to be very difficult but can and will change the course of your life for the better. You have to ask yourself, "Is the work worth getting the life I want, or do I accept the life I'm currently stuck with?"

If it's not worth it, that's okay. I prefer you say, "I'm not willing to do the work" instead of being the person who says you will do the work but don't actually do it.

All of this book will be useful in breaking objections and pitfalls that commonly happen when navigating change. You will be met with unknown unknowns. You will be met with doubts. You will be met with fear and uncertainty and maladaptive language from that lizard part of your brain that lies to you and tells you this is too hard or this is dumb.

We've been conditioned by too many movies showing drastic transformations in 90 minutes and now social media stories that wrap up transformations in 60 seconds. These are not real timelines. They do not show the effort, struggle, and amount of time change takes.

If you are willing to remove the expectations of easy and immediate and replace them with everyday action and commitment to changing course, you will create what you've always wished would somehow happen.

Somehow and someway are just a mask for your decisions and actions.

Once you've finally created the change you want, the work isn't over. Then it's time to be a beacon for others who are trying to do the same thing. More on that coming up in the next chapter.

## Pitfall 3: You Choose to Stay Stuck in One of the Phases

This pitfall is the most damaging as it gives you the illusion of progress, highlighting what you are doing but masking the areas you are ignoring.

As a person with diabetes, my blood sugar can go high for a variety of reasons. I've caught myself taking my medication late and getting high blood sugar even though I ate healthy, exercise regularly, drank enough water, had great blood sugar levels all day, and did all the other work!

The work you are actively doing does not make up for the work you are not doing.

If you answer 50 questions 100% right on a test, you still fail. The goal is not to blame or shame you for what you did not do, but equally the goal is not to use validation as to why half efforts should solve whole problems. Although honesty is part of Step 1, you need to be honest with yourself in assessing where you are in the process and whether you are resistant to a specific part of the process.

Have you gotten to the core issue? Have you faced the issues you are ready to fix? Are you holding yourself accountable to taking action? Are you getting accountability from someone else? Are you day by day improving your language, beliefs, actions, and progress? Are you living and acting as a role model you'd want your kids (or dogs) to have?

Don't fall into one of the following phase traps.

## STUCK IN SUBCONSCIOUS → CONSCIOUS PHASE

People who get stuck here often find themselves journaling, sometimes to the root of the issue and sometimes only superficially. Maybe they just constantly remind themselves of the problems or lean into the awareness of what the issues are.

Awareness is a fantastic first step (which is why it's our first step), but when you find yourself only taking one step in the right direction, you stay stuck in the wrong location. It doesn't matter how many times you repeat that first step, doing more of the same thing doesn't change anything.

Be the person who takes 10,000 steps in the right direction, not the person who repeats the same step 10,000 times.

## STUCK IN CONSCIOUS → COMMUNICATED PHASE

You are probably all too familiar with people who get stuck in this phase. They have successfully brought the real issues to the surface. They are ready to move on to Phase 2 and decide to talk to someone. Maybe it's a therapist or maybe it's a friend or even a partner. The problem is thinking awareness and communication for accountability are enough to course correct.

I had a friend who had been in therapy for years, and I originally applauded them for being vulnerable enough to seek out that inner honesty with someone else. Over the years, I noticed their constant struggle with perfectionism and lack of action other than speaking to their therapist.

It became apparent to me that that act of communicating and accountability warped into a false sense of progress for them, mutating therapy into the goal rather than the tool that needs to be actively utilized to get to the goal.

Whether it is therapy or accountability or communicating with someone you respect, change requires you to be an active participant in the process. Without willingness to do the work, both accountability and the *Art of Changing Course* can help you about as much as having a bank account with no money in it in hopes you become a millionaire. And while that might sound outlandish and pretty dumb, some people get stuck in this phase wondering why their mental bank account is empty of funds that they never put in there in the first place.

Be careful not to just be aware of your problems and feel as though telling someone else removes your own responsibility to act.

## STUCK IN COMMUNICATED → BROADCASTED PHASE

If you get stuck here, you are really close, but being close is just more frustrating than anything. You've successfully communicated your struggles not only to yourself but to others, and now you are ready to go on living and leading by example.

You make a specific to-do list, and damn does it feel good to have an action plan ready to go. All the effort in preparation to make the changes is present. The intention to act is there. But failure to translate intention into action docks more ships than storms.

I have hundreds of to-do lists in my notes section on my phone. I make to-do lists for everything, but when I get too busy or distracted, I tend to not complete my to-do lists, so I just rewrite them and add a to-do list on my to-do list. Planning to act feels good as it projects the desired state of life we want.

In writing the action plan, you almost borrow the feeling of success you'd get from doing the action by simply writing it down. That feeling is nice. But as we said, not all feelings are facts. Instead of letting your feelings drive you to repeatedly plan the action with sometimes no follow-through, let your discipline and accountability drive you to act daily.

Completing the tasks might suck now but feel great later. Avoiding the tasks might feel good now but suck later.

Both your action and lack of action are preparing you for the life ahead of you. Will you be proud of the course you're on, or do you need to change course?

You will be tempted to get stuck on the easiest part of the process. It doesn't mean you did it. Getting unstuck in life does not happen by repeating part of the process a million times—it happens by doing the full process (even the hard stuff and the parts you aren't great at) one solid time. The course you really want to be on has no room for half-truths or half-commitments, which act as the deadly sirens of the sea, telling you, "You did it" while you wait for the change that will never come.

"A half-truth is the worst of all lies, because it can be defended in partiality."

—*Solon the Athenian*

**Dorothy:** But, how do I start for Emerald City?

**Glinda:** It's always best to start at the beginning—and all you do is follow the Yellow Brick Road.

# CHAPTER 12

# Mentoring Others

Imagine Dorothy didn't sponsor change. If instead of inspiring the scarecrow, the lion, and the tinman, she either gave up on herself or selfishly didn't help those around her. Maybe that book would be titled *The Wizard of Modern-Day Selfishness* instead of *The Wizard of Oz*.

Dorothy's commitment to her mission and overcoming her perceived deficiencies mirrored as mentorship for the others, empowering and encouraging them to not only follow her but create their own path. She empowered them both directly and indirectly to their goal, yes, but also their truest desires: self-realization and personal growth.

If it weren't for Dorothy correcting her own course, the Lion, Tin Man, and Scarecrow likely would have remained stuck in their own self-doubt, immobilized by their language, perceived limitations, and lack of accountability.

We all know Dorothy helped the others change course and find resolution. The real question, though, is this: Would Dorothy have been successful in her own mission if she hadn't helped the others?

People tend to be selfish and think only about themselves.

Now, I am a huge proponent of the ideology that being selfish is necessary to be selfless. You have to take care of yourself before you give away everything you have to everyone else.

There is definitely a heathy version of self-interest you should maintain, but when that self-interest undermines your relationships, community, or organization, we have a problem.

Why have we lost track of doing our part in our lives for the world?

Because we're busy? Because we're stressed? Because of whatever?

Maybe it's the rise in individualism and entrepreneurship. Maybe it's a culture shift to a "me first" approach. Maybe we are just so focused on keeping our head above water that anyone in our way is collateral damage.

Whatever the reason, it's imperative that you understand the reasons and benefits of both acting like a mentor and actively being a mentor for others.

The final step in the art of changing course is broadcasting your change and improved processes, becoming a potential mentor for others to follow. Now, that mentorship can be taken by others passively or actively.

People may subconsciously pick up on your behaviors and be inspired to replicate that for their own life. And in that way, you are not doing much more than existing as your best self, knowing people are watching. But what about actively deciding to be a mentor? What is the role or benefit of mentoring others when it comes to you and your progress?

There is a big difference between living as a role model and choosing to mentor others directly. I would argue that being a role model in your relationship, organization, and life should be a bare minimum requirement. Not only is it a positive influence on others, but it also helps hold your accountability to continually be the person you've become and not backtrack.

Deciding to mentor someone directly is much more external. Role models are expected to lead by example. Mentors are expected to lead, teach, guide, support, and help those under them. There is a lot more responsibility that comes with mentoring others. So, to be quite direct, why would you actively take on more responsibility? What's in it for you?

Not many people know that Steve Jobs acted as a mentor for Mark Zuckerberg in the early years of Facebook. Steve and Mark were often seen taking walks together in Palo Alto, discussing everything from developing a management team to reconnecting with Mark's original mission when things went awry. Steve was able to mentor Mark through the challenges of managing a rapidly growing company.

But mentorship is not a one-way street. In mentoring one of the biggest disruptors of social interaction, Steve was able to reflect on his own processes and management styles, likely influencing his approach to running the tech giant Apple. Other immeasurable benefits of that mentorship may include his fulfillment in assisting like-minded people, sharpening his own practices, testing problem-solving strategies, and more.

Mentorship benefits all involved, encouraging reciprocity to and from the mentor. Prosocial behavior, or actions meant to help others, is shown to increase happiness, fulfillment, and overall motivation (Miles et al. 2022). Mentoring others is a form of prosocial behavior that overall just benefits you as a person and/or leader. Through your interaction with your mentees, you get to enhance your social skills, leadership skills, and problem-solving skills while likely improving your sense of fulfillment and satisfaction in life.

What better way to stay motivated and unstuck than to mentor others to better parts of their lives while you get a heaping number of rewards yourself. There is nothing wrong with personally benefiting from helping others.

Now, like an opportunity for gain in life, mentorship has one potential downfall. You cannot fully rely on yourself to make the mentorship successful. This presents a problem if your mentee decides not to commit or falls short.

Luckily the problem is not your mentees' decisions but rather your reactions to their decisions.

It doesn't matter whether you are the CEO or the best friend or the camp counselor; your job is to give whatever good you can to your mentee. And in giving that good, you are successful in your mentorship.

Where you might go wrong is if you base your success on their decisions and actions.

It's tempting not set boundaries in the process of helping other people. One of the most frustrating feelings in the world is wanting results for someone more than they want it for themselves.

This is why it's important to set boundaries in regard to what your job is and what your job is not.

You are there as a mentor to provide support and guidance.

You are not there to belittle them or yell at them for their actions.

You are their mentor, not their parent.

If they choose not to do the work, the mentorship ends. It's that simple. No fighting, convincing, or pleading required. If you are not put in a position to successfully do your job, then that job is not for you.

No reason to get mad when expectations are not met and boundaries are crossed.

But for those who choose to show up and do the work, that's where the benefits of mentorship will shine through all walks of your life (and theirs).

Successful mentorship reinforces your best behaviors while refining your ability to spot language limitations, honest ownership of problems, and needs for accountable action.

In essence, by mentoring others, you fortify your decision to never stay stuck again.

Sometimes we just need a catalyst to change. And other times we need to be the catalyst for change.

Dorothy was a catalyst for her group. But what if she wasn't?

If Dorothy weren't the catalyst, what would have happened? Would they have just waited for someone else to help? Why wait for change when you can be the change?

Why not be the lighthouse and help others find their way?

A lot of people are looking for a Dorothy in their own story. But why not stop looking for Dorothy and be Dorothy? Dorothy didn't have a Dorothy. She helped countless other people, and countless people are thankful because of her.

You can wait and wait for someone to rescue you as I did for 17 years. Or you can start becoming what you need.

The Scarecrow and Lion and Tin Man didn't "need" Dorothy. But she sure helped them find the change they were looking for a lot faster.

Becoming a Dorothy helps society and you as a person maintain and sustain change.

In the corporate world, when you're a change champion or sponsoring change you help everyone maintain change. You're helping yourself, others, and your organization. You're helping yourself, people you love, and people you don't know to help themselves. It's a domino effect of impact.

One of the classic studies in social psychology is the Solomon Asch conformity line experiment. In it, groups of people were asked to simply identify which two lines on a card matched each other in length. Each group included only one real subject, while the others had been prompted to give the incorrect answer. Researchers found that even though the answer was obvious, 75 percent of participants conformed with the majority in at least one of the clinical trials. The impact of others (even strangers) can affect not only how we answer questions to problems that seem obvious but how we choose to respond to all problems.

What are your worst habits teaching others? In your organization with your employees or in your home with your family, you inspire people to be like you. As it stands right now, is that a good thing or a bad thing?

In all we do, we are serving as a model for others. People pay attention to what we do and put a lot of weight on how we respond to problems that arise.

Whether it's kids looking up to you as a role model or adults sharing space with you at home or work, people see what you go through and how you act. When you start working through the Changing Course process, you learn to start treating your reactions and decisions with care as they influence your world and the world around you.

You become a lighthouse for other people, whether you want to be or not.

When you engage in prosocial behavior by thinking about how you can benefit others, it also helps you. Researchers have found that subjects who spent more time engaged in prosocial behavior showed higher levels of positive mood and were able to handle daily stress more smoothly.

By taking ownership of your problems and working through this process to change course, you never know just how many lives you may change as a result.

Dorothy didn't have to learn how to be Dorothy. Scarecrow didn't have to learn how to get brains. He just had to be put in a position to prove that he already had it.

Again: Ships are safest in the harbor, but that's not what ships are built for. If you put yourself in a position to not use your brains, of course you're going to doubt you have brains.

The benefits outweigh the cost. Improving the areas in your life that bring you the most amount of grief, struggle, angst, stagnation, and resistance not only can drastically improve your quality of life and help you progress contentedly toward a life you're proud of, but also your commitment to your improvement flashes like a rescue beacon to everyone around you. Everyone close to you personally and professionally—everyone struggling with similar problems—will learn from you not what you teach or tell but rather what to do based on what *you* do.

How amazing is it that by merely putting in the honest work to change and get unstuck, that effort can serve as inspiration to your team and people around you to do the exact same thing. You don't need to be a perfect role model. You don't need to have 100% mastered your change. You don't need to become superhuman. You just need to put the honest effort in to change the habits and processes that are doing more damage than good.

If I waited to start my speaking career until I was a perfect example of mental fortitude and confidence, I would have never started. Hundreds of thousands of people would have missed out on my message. Certain company culture shifts might have never happened. Thousands of kids wouldn't have seen that "cool guy with a disability just like me" on TV with The Rock. And I'd still be waiting for perfection that you know never actually comes. In starting my speaking career from a place of vulnerability, sharing my expertise without hiding the areas I was actively working on, I was able to take my people, my audience, my clients, my world with me as I changed the course of my life. Choosing authenticity over perfection helped me grow as a person and as a leader. Choosing to share my journey before I was perfect allowed me to connect with people as everyone can relate.

Getting it perfect and then leading is just avoidance and imposter syndrome rearing its head saying, "You are not good enough yet." As you know by now, feelings aren't facts. Live by example and perfect as you go. You can always perfect the process, but you will never have a fully perfect process. Why? Because change can render perfect plans useless. But change can't stop you from your own internal efforts to commit to your constant growth.

Are you living your life as the person you needed most at your darkest time? Are you leading people as the leader you wish you had at your lowest point? How different would your choices be if you started behaving the way your ideal version of yourself would behave?

Similar to turning the steering wheel or trimming the sail, altering your course requires action. Sustaining that course requires a commitment to action. Enjoying that course requires helping others do the same thing.

It's never too late to change, and it's never too soon to start.

# References

Brinthaupt, Thomas M., and Alain Morin. (2023). "Self-talk: Research Challenges and Opportunities." *Frontiers in Psychology* 14. https://doi.org/10.3389/fpsyg.2023.1210960. PMID: 37465491; PMCID: PMC10350497.

Burnes, Bernard. (2020). "The Origins of Lewin's Three-Step Model of Change." *The Journal of Applied Behavioral Science* 56(1): 32–59. https://doi.org/10.1177/0021886319892685.

Cohn Jr., Samuel K. (2018). *Epidemics: Hate and Compassion from the Plague of Athens to AIDS*. Oxford University Press.

Fogg, B. J. (2019). *Tiny Habits: The Small Changes That Change Everything*. Eamon Dolan Books.

Gibson, Alan St. Clair, and Carl Foster. (2007). "The Role of Self-Talk in the Awareness of Physiological State and Physical Performance." *Sports Medicine* 37, 1029–1044. https://doi.org/10.2165/00007256-200737120-00003. PMID: 18027992.

Hsu, Tzu-Yu, Tzu-Ling Liu, Paul Z. Cheng, Hsin-Chien Lee, Timothy J. Lane, and Niall W. Duncan. (2021). "Depressive Rumination Is Correlated with Brain Responses during Self-Related Processing." *Journal of Psychiatry and Neuroscience* 46, no. 5 (2021): E518–E527. https://doi.org/10.1503/jpn.210052. Epub 2021 Sep 1. PMID: 34548386; PMCID: PMC8526127.

Johnson, Spencer. (1998). *Who Moved My Cheese*. G. P. Putnam's Sons.

Jung, Carl. (1963). *Memories, Dream, Reflections*. Pantheon Books.

Kennedy, J. F. (1962). "Commencement Address at Yale University." The American Presidency Project, 11.

Miles, Andrew, Meena Andiappan, Laura Upenieks, and Christos Orfanidis. "Using Prosocial Behavior to Safeguard Mental Health and Foster Emotional Well-Being during the COVID-19 Pandemic: A Registered Report of a Randomized Trial." *PloS one* 17, no. 7 (2022): e0272152.

Moser, Jason S., Adrienne Dougherty, Whitney I. Mattson, Benjamin Katz, Tim P. Moran, Darwin Guevarra, Holly Shablack et al. "Third-Person Self-Talk Facilitates Emotion Regulation without Engaging Cognitive Control: Converging Evidence from ERP and fMRI." *Scientific Reports* 7, no. 1 (2017): 4519. https://doi.org/10.1038/s41598-017-04047-3.

Robert, Ellen R., and Gregg Thomson. (1994). "Learning Assistance and the Success of Underrepresented Students at Berkeley." *Journal of Developmental Education* 17(3): 4.

Rumsfeld, D. 2002. Defense Briefing. Defense.gov. "News Transcript: DoD News Briefing—Secretary Rumsfeld and Gen. Myers." United States Department of Defense. February 12, 2002. Archived from the original on April 6, 2016. https://web.archive.org/web/20160406235718/http://archive.defense.gov/Transcripts/Transcript.aspx?TranscriptID=2636.

Savion, Leah (2009). "Clinging to Discredited Beliefs: The Larger Cognitive Story." *Journal of the Scholarship of Teaching and Learning* 9(1): 81–92.

Tavris, Carol, and Elliot Aronson. (2007). *Mistakes Were Made (But Not by Me): Why We Justify Foolish Beliefs, Bad Decisions, and Harmful Acts*. Harcourt.

Tversky, Amos, and Daniel Kahneman. (1974). "Judgment under Uncertainty: Heuristics and Biases: Biases in Judgments Reveal Some Heuristics of Thinking under Uncertainty." *Science* 185(4157): 1124–1131. https://doi.org/10.21236/ad0767426.

# About the Author

When I was born, my left arm was shorter than my right and ended with only two fingers instead of five. I still remember when I finally worked up the nerve to ask out Crystal, the prettiest girl in school. She responded by picking up a stapler and miming my arm, calling me "club boy." Bullying like this continued mercilessly and caused me such humiliation that I took to hiding my hand in my pocket or in a glove for 17 years. This caused a lot of logistical issues. If I accidentally put my hand in my pocket through my backpack strap, I would have to ask to go to the bathroom to take my backpack off. I once got beat up on the beach because I wouldn't take my hand out of my pocket. And then of course there was the time I almost got arrested in Washington, DC, because I wouldn't take my hand out of my pocket for security.

When I was 19, I was diagnosed with type 1 diabetes. Falling in love with doing things people told me I couldn't, I decided that I wanted to get into bodybuilding. I won my very first powerlifting competition and then the next six after that. People started to take notice of this young kid with a glove and special lifting hook (which I had worked with a company to develop), and I started building a name for myself on social media.

From there, I had a successful personal training business but eventually grew tired of the pure exercise focus. Fitness is easy in principle: Eat less, work out more, and boom—you'll lose weight and look good. But looking good and feeling good are two different things. Developing a healthy mentality based on authenticity and ownership was the challenge I wanted to help people address. I think I knew deep down that we all teach best what we need to learn, and that was me: this externally super-confident guy who was hiding in public.

I had developed a persona around my hidden disability; I was Chris, the guy with the glove. I played drums and put the drumstick through the finger hole of one of the gloves. I did breakdance. I was a record-holding powerlifter. No one questioned me perhaps because I was so outwardly confident. I told myself that if I ever got a prosthetic arm, maybe I would be able to stop hiding my hand. It's very difficult to get a prosthetic arm, especially as an adult, so this felt like a safe promise to make. I was wrong.

When I was approved for my prosthetic, I knew I had to make good on what I had promised myself. I filmed a video and asked my then-girlfriend of four and a half years to edit it. It was the first time in our relationship that she had ever seen my hand. I woke up the next morning to a flood of views and messages. That video has now been viewed millions of times. What I later realized was that while that was a big moment, there had been hundreds of decisions and conversations that had led to it.

To be fair, I was doing cool stuff and seeing success even before I stopped hiding.

However, the opportunities have really exploded since I posted that video. I was invited to do a TV show with The Rock, had a two-page spread in *People Magazine*, and have spoken to audiences of tens of thousands, just to name a few. Opening up about my problems has allowed me to connect with people from all over the world. At the end of the day, what I was most afraid of ended up becoming the best thing in my life.

# Index

Acceptance, 8
  for contentment, 22
  of feedback, 179–185
  of full responsibility, 81
  problem-solving matrix
      for, 87–88
  radical, 89
  rules for, 86–87
  in Subconscious to
      Conscious step, 85, 86
  of your true self, 102
Accountability, 11
  communication for, 181–183
  in Conscious to
      Communicated step,
      106–107, 125–131
  for effective change, 123
  in the wrong direction, 182
  to yourself, 106–107
Accountability
      devices, 127–128
Accountability partners, 127
Action(s):
  accountability for, 125–131
  barrier to, 118
  celebrating, 150–152
  commitment to, 57–58,
      115–117, 206

  to correct issues, 181
  knowledge vs., 184
  responsibility for, 196
  separating your identity
      from, 137–139
  taking, 79–81, 101, 206
  that stick, 160
Action plans, 196–197
Acute stuckness, 47–49
Adaptability, 106,
      143, 168–171
Addressing stuckness, 27–39
  ambiguity effect in, 34–35
  anchoring effect in, 35–36
  belief perseverance in,
      36–39
  loss aversion in, 33–34
  mindset for, 28
  positivity in, 29
  resistance to, 30–31
  sunk-cost fallacy in, 32–33
  zero-sum bias in, 32
Agricultural Revolution,
      169–170
AI (artificial intelligence),
      43–44
Alcoholics Anonymous,
      122, 157

All Great and Powerful Oz
(in *Wizard of Oz*),
9, 82, 164
Amazon, 176
Ambiguity effect, 34–35
Americans with Disabilities
Act, Section 504, 136
Amygdala, 33–34
Anchoring effect, 34–36
Apple Pay, 78, 201
Aronson, Elliot, 37
Artificial intelligence
(AI), 43–44
Asch, Solomon, 203
Asking for help, 112–115,
114*t*, 183
Association for Talent
Development, 126
Authenticity, perfection
vs., 205
Automobile industry, 170
Avoidance mechanisms,
55, 191, 205
Avon, 175

Barefoot King story, 78–79
Baum, L. Frank, 8
Behavior modeling. *See also*
Communicated to
Broadcast (Step 3)
as being a lighthouse,
153–159, 204
intentional and
unintentional, 153
through mentoring, 199–206

of your best self, 65
Beliefs:
about yourself, 45, 110,
133
biases perpetuated by, 49
broadcasting, 154
"certainty" about, 141
changing your, 138
commitment to, 19
and language/dialogue,
50, 51, 54
limiting, 58, 144
and stuckness, 45
unrealistic, 139
Belief perseverance, 36–39
Best Buy, 176
Bitcoin, 118
BlackBerry, 177
Blockbuster, 176, 177
Boundaries, 202
Brain:
default mode network
in, 50, 51
encoding in, 99, 100
familiarity and comfort
sought by, 30
and helping others,
113
language processing and
generation in, 44
lizard part of, 191, 194
and loss aversion, 33–34
neuroplasticity of, 51
Broadcasting:
of your changes, 200

of your problems, 181 (*See also* Communicated to Broadcast (Step 3))
Buddha, 49
Bureaucracy, 176
The Buy Guide, 180

Cannon, Taylor, 179–180
Celebrating change/success, 58, 137, 150–152
Certainty, 141–143, 143*t*
Certainty mindset, 146
Change, 3–9, 11, 22–23
  celebrating, 137, 150–152
  creating environments conducive to, 14 (*See also* Changing Course process)
  fear of, 30–31
  finding stability in, 22
  habituation as, 147
  importance of brain in, 52–53
  life as, 168
  major contributors to, 123
  permission to, 63–73
  prescription for, 63–73
  psychological barriers to, 67 (*See also specific barriers*)
  resistance to (*see* Resistance to change)
  Three Step Model of, 11
  "trying everything" for, 52

wanting vs. working for, 29
willingness for, 31, 49
Change management:
  classic study of, 8 (*See also The Wonderful Wizard of Oz* (Baum))
  with disruptive change, 6 (*See also specific topics*)
  as revolving door, 159
Change step, 11. *See also* Accountability
Changing Course process, 7, 11
  for health, 171–172
  issues addressed by, 162
  mentoring others in, 199–206
  and organizational factors in stuckness, 175–177
  pitfalls in, 187–197
  real-world application of, 167–177
  for relationships, 173–175
  shifts in, 11
  solving core problem in, 12–14
  steps in, 12–14 (*See also individual steps*)
  underlying principles, techniques, and theories for, 11
  for wealth, 172–173
ChatGPT, 43–44, 47
Cherry-picking, 44, 169

Choices, subpar, 149–150
Chronic stuckness, 47–49
Civil rights, 154
Cognitive dissonance, 36
Cognitive restructuring, 49
Cohn, Samuel K., Jr., 167
Comfort, 30
  change as threat to, 30
  rationalizing certainty
      for, 141–142
  seeking, 190–191
  with your identity, 30
Commitment(s):
  competing, 67–69,
      68*t*, 115–119
  cost of overcommitting,
      120–123
  half-, 197
  as inspiration to
      others, 204–205
  outcome-based goals
      vs., 119–120
  to process vs. to
      mission, 189
Communicated to Broadcast
      (Step 3), 13–14, 135–164
  behavior modeling
      in, 153–159
  being stuck in, 196–197
  celebrating change
      in, 150–152
  certainty in, 141–143, 143*t*
  curiosity in, 142–143, 143*t*
  effort vs. perfection
      in, 148–150

  and identity
      protection, 137–140
  living by example in,
      140–141
  and perfectionism, 159–162
  thinking outside the box in,
      143–148, 144*f*, 145*f*
Communication:
  accepting feedback,
      179–185
  during pandemics, 168
  of your problem, 123–125
Competence, 30, 55, 56*f*
Competing commitments/
      goals, 67–69,
      68*t*, 115–119
Complacency, 177
Confirmation bias, 168
Conformity line
      experiment, 203
Connectedness, 107–108. *See
      also* Conscious to
      Communicated (Step 2)
Conscious to Communicated
      (Step 2), 13, 105–133
  accountability in, 106–107,
      125–131
  and asking for help,
      112–115, 114*t*
  being stuck in, 195–196
  commitment in, 115–119
  communicating your
      problem in, 123–125
  and cost of overcommitting,
      120–123

cultural influences in, 109
educational influences in,
110
and outcome-based
goals, 119–120
and self-reliance, 107–108
social influences in, 109–110
workplace influences
in, 110–112
Contentment, 22, 113
Control, desire for, 30, 31
Core problem:
addressing, 27–39
discovery process for, 88–89
identifying, 17–25
solving, 12–14 (*See also*
Changing Course
process)
symptoms of, 18
Covey, Stephen, 123
Cultural influences, 108, 109
Curiosity, 142–143, 143*t*

Dead Sea, 162
Deceit, 87
DEI (diversity, equity, and
inclusion), 12, 13
Demand, induced, 19
Dereniowski, Zachery, 112–113
Desire points, 5
*Dhammapada*, 49
Digital media, 170–171
Disabilities:
adaptive clothing
for, 156–157

fear of, 10
owning, 10
physical, 10, 21
rights of people
with, 135–136
Discovery process, 88–89
Dishonesty, 86
Disruptive change, 6–7
managing, 6 (*See also
specific topics*)
and negative rumination/
thoughts, 50
pain from, 89–90
Diversity, equity, and
inclusion (DEI), 12, 13
Donkey Kong, 85
Dorothy (in *Wizard of Oz*), 8
on being home, 166
as example/mentor,
199, 202, 203
on keeping promises, 82
on killing the witch, 74
and Lion's fear, 62
on Miss Gulch, 178
on missing Lion, 134
on needing help, 104
and reality of the
wizard, 164
and Scarecrow's
problem, 16
on starting for Emerald
City, 198
steps taken toward
Oz by, 161
Dorsey, John, 138–139

Easiness:
  simplicity vs., 193–194
  of staying stuck,
    180–181
Educational influences, 110
Effort, perfection vs.,
    148–150
Ego:
  defensive, 90–91
  familiarity and comfort
    sought by, 30
  and fear of change, 30–31
  and resistance to new
    evidence, 37
Electricity, rise of, 170
Example, living by, *see* Living
  by example
Excruciating the details,
    94–96
External change, 3, 6

Facebook, 201
Facts:
  biases and effects
    contradicting, 32–39
  feelings vs., 45
  language based in, 45
Failure:
  avoiding, 34
  fear of, 110
  riskiness of, 191
  from scaling ineffective
    systems, 18–20
  vulnerability as admission
    of, 31

Familiarity:
  desire to maintain, 5, 30
    (*See also* Resistance
      to change)
  of prior commitments, 118
  security of, 31
  in self-reliance, 111–112
Fear:
  of being alone, 21
  of disabilities, 9
  of failing after
    getting help, 110
  of threats to ego, 30
Feedback, accepting, 179–185
Feedback loop, 19, 51
Feelings, 21, 22, 45.
    *See also* Fear
Five Whys technique,
    91–94, 92*f*
Fixed mindset, 100

Gatorade, 43
Giving, asking for help as,
    112–115, 114*t*
Glinda (in *Wizard of Oz*),
    104, 198
Goals:
  accountability for, 126
  competing, 67–69, 68*t*
  outcome-based, 119–120
  reasonable, 120–123
  small steps toward, 118–119
  written, 99
Goggins, David, 41–42
@goob_u2, 138–139

Gratification, 192–193
Growth, 8, 152

Habits:
  changing your phrasing
      around, 53
  for creating change, 14
      (*See also* Changing
      Course process)
  living the life created
      by, 136
  others impacted by, 203
  possibility for changing, 42
  separating your identity
      from, 137–139
  that reflect best or ideal
      self, 65, 140
Habituation, 146–147
Hawthorne effect, 129
Health, making changes in,
      71–73, 171–172
Help:
  asking for and giving,
      112–115, 114*t*, 183
      (*See also* Conscious
      to Communicated
      (Step 2))
  refusing or avoiding, 106
  and self-reliance, 107–108
  setting boundaries on, 202
Heraclitus, 23
Hierarchy, organizational, 176
Highway systems, 19–20
Hippocampus, 99
Holmes, Elizabeth, 32

Homer, 187–188
Honesty:
  about where you are, 101
  in language, 44–47
  need for, 183
  resistance to, 31
  rules for, 86–87
  with yourself, 11, 181 (*See
      also* Subconscious to
      Conscious (Step 1))
Hsieh, Tony, 156–157
Huemann, Judy, 135–136
Hunk (in *Wizard of Oz*), 178
Hutchinson, Linley, 179–180

Ideal self:
  individuality of, 163
  living as your, 158 (*See also*
      Living by example)
  reflecting your, 140
Identifying core
      problems, 17–25
Identity:
  comfort with your, 30
  confusing habits
      with, 137–140
Imposter syndrome, 205
Induced demand, 19
Industrial Revolution, 170
Initiating change, 4, 49
Insular cortex, 34
Interdependence, 107–108.
      *See also* Conscious to
      Communicated
      (Step 2)

Internal change, 3
  disruptive, 6–7
  self-talk, 49
  unmasking issues
      preventing, 89–92
Internal language/dialog/
      narrative, 43, 49–61, 56*f*
  and brain function, 50–52
  celebrating
      corrections of, 151
  in changing habits, 53
  in Linguistic Matrix for
      Change, 54–61, 56*f*
  and monkey mind, 49
  negative, 50, 51
  self-talk, 42
Irrational escalation, 32

Job dissatisfaction, 69–70
Jobs, Steve, 201
Johnson, Dwayne
      "The Rock," 10
Johnson, Spencer, 75–76
Jordan, Michael, 46
Journaling, 99–103
Jung, Carl, 96

Kahneman, Daniel, 35
Katy Freeway, 20
Kennedy, John F., 46
Keyes, Jim, 177
King, Martin Luther, Jr., 155
Know-it-all mindset, 28
Knowledge, 28
  action vs., 184

certainty vs., 141
implementation
    vs., 192–193
willingness to be
    wrong about, 43
Known knowns, 27
Known unknowns, 27, 28
Kodak, 176
Kutol, 84

Language, 41–61
  and chronic vs. acute
      stuckness, 47–49
  and fear of the
      unknown, 31
  importance of, 46
  ineffective, 142
  internal, 43, 49–61, 56*f*
      (*See also* Internal
      language/dialog/
      narrative)
  of lies vs. facts, 45–47
  and misinformation, 44
  and self-talk, 42
  and strategies that maintain
      stuckness, 45
Leaders:
  behavior modeling
      by, 155–156
  great, 9
  mindset for, 28
Learn-it-all mindset, 28
LeSueur, Ashlee, 179–180
Lewin, Kurt, 11
Lewis, C.S., 39

Lies:
  about having tried
    everything, 61
  changing phrasing
    about, 53–54
  comfortable, 141–142
  facts vs., 45
  language based in, 45
  to yourself, 53–54, 130
Lifestyle changes, 71–73
Limiting beliefs, 58, 144
Linguistic Matrix for Change,
  54–61, 56*f*
  almost there quadrant of,
    56*f*, 59–61
  change maker quadrant of,
    57–58, 56*f*
  know it all; do it naught
    quadrant of, 57, 56*f*
  the stuck quadrant
    of, 56*f*, 58
Lion (in *Wizard of Oz*),
  8, 60
  accountability for, 131
  on courage, 40
  Dorothy's example
    for, 199, 203
  fear of, 62
  on finding courage, 134
  on monkey's attacks, 186
  on Scarecrow's problem-
    solving, 26
  steps taken toward
    Oz by, 161
*The Little Mermaid*, 83–84

Living by example, 11,
  140–141, 152. *See also*
  Communicated to
  Broadcast (Step 3)
Loss aversion, 33–34, 54
Louis XVI, King of France, 66

McVicker, Joe, 84
"Man in a hole" stories,
  84–85
Maraboli, Steve, 130
@mdmotivator, 112–113
*Men's Health*, 10
Mentoring others, 199–206
Merton, Thomas, 15
Metabole, 23. *See also* Change
Microwaves, 142
Mindset:
  of certainty, 146
  feeling stuck with, 6
  fixed, 100
  know-it-all vs.
    learn-it-all, 28
  of making a one-degree
    difference, 159–162
  of self-reliance, 107–108
  and self-talk, 42
Mission, 189–190
Missteps/mistakes:
  as excuse for future
    mistakes, 149
  owning up to, 13 (*See also*
    Conscious to
    Communicated (Step 2))
  repeating, 22

*Mistakes Were Made (But Not by Me)* (Tavris and Aronson), 37

*Mister Rogers' Neighborhood*, 155

Monkey mind, 49

Motivation(s):
  for change, 5, 123
  to commit and track progress, 107
  from helping others, 201

Motley Fool, 177

Narcotics Anonymous, 157

Narratives, 42, 112. *See also* Language

Negative thoughts, 49, 76

Netflix, 10, 43, 54, 177

Neurolinguistic programming, 53

Neuroplasticity, 51

*New York Times*, 20

Nike, 10, 156

Nine-dot exercise, 143–148, 144*f*, 145*f*

Nintendo, 84–85

Normalizing dysfunctional patterns, 106

*The Odyssey* (Homer), 187–188

*On Certainty* (Wittgenstein), 141

One-degree shift, 159–162

Optimism, 29

Organizations, stuckness in, 175–177

Outcome-based goals, 119–120

Outside-the-box thinking, 143–148, 144*f*, 145*f*

Overcommitment, 120–123

Overworking, 110–112

Ovington, Mary White, 154

Ownership:
  of disabilities, 10
  of missteps/mistakes, 13 (*See also* Conscious to Communicated (Step 2))
  of real problems, 89–90
  of where you are, 101

Pain:
  adapting to, 106
  avoiding, 85
  from disruptive change, 89–90
  from yourself, 54

Pain points, 5

Pandemics, 167–169

Parks, Rosa, 154

Perfection:
  choosing authenticity over, 205
  effort vs., 148–150
  one-degree shift from, 159–162

Permission:
  to change, 63–73
  to stay stuck, 66

Perspective, choosing, 60–61

Physical disabilities, 10, 21
Pitfalls in changing, 187–197
  knowing what you need
    without implementing
    it, 192–193
  seeing simplicity as
    easiness, 193–194
  staying stuck in one
    phase, 194–197
Play-Doh, 84
Positivity, 29
Prescription for change, 63–73
  giving yourself permission
    to change, 63–73
  scenarios of, 69–73
Presley, Elvis, 35
Problem-solving, 12–14. *See
    also* Changing
    Course process
  bringing things to the
    surface for, 100–103
  effective, 95–96
  matrix for, 88
  nine-dot exercise, 143–148,
    144*f*, 145*f*
Procrastination, 55
Projections, 96
Prosocial behavior,
    158, 201, 204

Racism, 155
Radio Shack, 175–176
Radmacher, Mary Anne, 162
Raytheon, 142
Reacting to change, 4, 5

Realism, 29
Reality, 85–88, 132
Redbox, 177
Reframing, 53
Refreezing step, 11. *See also*
    Living by example
Reinvention, 6
Relationships, making changes
    in, 70–71, 163, 173–175
Repression, 97
Research in Motion, 177
Resistance to change:
  ambiguity effect in, 34–35
  anchoring effect in, 35–36
  belief
    perseverance in, 36–39
  ego in, 30–31
  loss aversion in, 33–34
  in organizations, 175
  from prior commitments,
    116–117
  realization of, 99
  signs of, 91
  sunk-cost fallacy in, 32–33
  zero-sum bias in, 32
Responsibility, 80
  accepting, 81
  to act, 196
  for fixing problems, 13
    (*See also* Conscious to
    Communicated (Step 2))
  for problems, 12 (*See also*
    Subconscious to
    Conscious (Step 1))
  and validation, 182

Risk aversion, 176
Robbins, Tony, 14
Rogers, Fred, 155
Role modeling, 11, 162,
    200–201. *See also*
    Behavior modeling
Roosevelt, Franklin D., 36
Root cause analysis,
    92–94, 92*f*
Root cause of problems, *see*
    Core problem
Rumsfeld, Donald, 27

Safety, seeking, 190–191, 204
Scaling ineffective
    systems, 18–20
Scapegoating, 167–168
Scarecrow (in *Wizard
    of Oz*), 8
    Dorothy's example
        for, 199, 203
    on Dorothy's need
        for help, 104
    language and self-talk of, 60
    and Lion's fear, 62
    on monkeys' attacks, 186
    problem of, 16
    problem-solving by, 26
    steps taken toward
        Oz by, 161
Schultz, Howard, 84
Schwartz, Tony, 140–141
Sea of Galilee, 162
Sears Roebuck Company,
    17–18, 177

Sears Tower, 17
See It, Fact It, Fix It, 75–81
    corporate example of, 75
    literary example of,
        75–76
    personal example of, 76–77
Self:
    acceptance of, 102
    accountability to, 106–107
    beliefs about, 45, 110, 133
    best possible version
        of, 147–148
    cherry-picking for or
        against, 44
    commitment as
        promise to, 115
    honesty with, 181
    ideal, 140, 153, 158
    real vs. false versions of, 10
Self-care, 107
Self-determination, 107–108
Self-interest, 199–200
Selfishness, 158, 199
Self-justification, 37, 38
Self-reliance, 107–108
Self-talk, 42, 48, 49. *See
    also* Language
Shadow work, 96–99
Simplicity, easiness
    vs., 193–194
Social influences, 107–110
Social media, behavior
    modeling via, 153–154
Societal issues, challenging,
    155

Sokolov, Evgeny, 146
Solon the Athenian, 197
Spencer, Percy, 142
Stability, 22
Stanley, William, 179
Stanley cups, 179–180
Starbucks, 84
Status, fear of losing, 30
Strategy, lack of, 175–176
Striatum, 34
Stuckness, 5–6
  addressing, 27–39
  chronic vs. acute, 47–49
  common causes of, 7,
    20–21
  core issue causing, 20 (*See
    also* Core problem)
  giving yourself permission
    for, 66–67
  investing in strategies that
    maintain, 45
  moving to reinvention
    from, 6
  organizational factors
    in, 175–177
  in a phase, 194–197
  in process of wanting to
    change, 191
  as repeating past
    mistakes, 22
  safety of, 190–191
  See It, Fact It, Fix It
    technique for,
    75–81
  story behind your, 31

Subconscious to Conscious
    (Step 1), 12, 83–103
  being stuck in, 195
  discovery process in,
    88–89
  excruciating the
    details in, 94–96
  Five Whys technique in,
    92–94, 92*f*
  identifying what exists
    in the shadows
    in, 96–99
  purpose of, 85–86
  rules for, 86–87
  unmasking the
    problem in, 89–92
  writing results in, 99–103
Success:
  celebrating, 58, 137,
    150–152
  complacency in, 177
  effective plan for, 59
  in mentorship, 202
  repeated, 151–152
Sunk-cost fallacy, 32–33
Support, asking for, 182.
    *See also* Help
Swift, Taylor, 17, 38
Systems, ineffective, 18–20

Tavris, Carol, 37
Taylor Swift Eras Tour, 17
Theranos, 32–33
Thinking outside the box,
    143–148, 144*f*, 145*f*

Thoughts. *See also* Internal
    language/dialog/
    narrative
  choosing your, 45
  getting lost in, 100
  importance of, 49–50
  negative, 49, 76
  and stuckness, 45
  unconscious, 96–98
Three Step Model of
    Change, 11
Tin Man (in *Wizard of Oz*), 8
  Dorothy's example
    for, 199, 203
  language and self-talk of, 60
  and Lion's fear, 62
  on monkey's attacks, 186
  steps taken toward
    Oz by, 161
  on what Dorothy
    learned, 104
*Titan Games*, 10
To-do lists, 196–197
Tommy Hilfiger, 10
Toxic help cycle, 133
Toyoda, Sakichi, 92
Toyota, 92
Toys R Us, 177
Transition periods, 171
Transportation systems, 19
Truth(s), 45–46
  certainty vs., 141
  half-, 197
  manipulating, 139, 141

  paradoxical, 115
  in Subconscious to
      Conscious step, 86
*Tsundoku*, 192
Tversky, Amos, 35
Twain, Mark, 87

Unconscious thoughts, 96–98
The UN Convention on the
    Rights of Persons with
    Disabilities, 136
Unfreezing step, 11. *See
    also* Honesty
Unknown, fear of, 31
Unknown unknowns, 27, 28
Unmasking the
    problem, 89–92

Validation, 105, 182
Vision, lack of, 175–176
Vulnerability, 30–31, 100, 124

Walgreens, 32–33
Walling, William English, 154
Walmart, 18
*The Washington Post*, 10
WD-40, 43
Wealth, making changes
    in, 172–173
*Who Moved My Cheese?*
    (Johnson), 75–76
Winfrey, Oprah, 154
Winning bias, 151–152
Wittgenstein, Ludwig, 141

*The Wonderful Wizard of Oz*
(Baum), 8, 131. *See also*
*individual characters*
characters'
challenges in, 188
language and self-talk of
characters in, 60
stuckness of
characters in, 21
Workplace:
influences in, 110–112
job dissatisfaction in, 69–70

making changes in, 163–164
Writing, reflecting
through, 99–103

Yamauchi, Hiroshi, 85
Yellow brick road,
29, 164–165
YouTube, 43–44

Zappos, 10, 156–157
Zero-sum bias, 32
Zuckerberg, Mark, 201